ANYTHING IS POSSIBLE

Fatima and Amna Sultan

Copyright © 2019 Sultan Akif

ISBN : 978-1-9993960-3-9

All rights reserved.

Fatima and Amna Sultan asserts their right to be identified as the author of this work. No part of this book may be reproduced, stored in or introduced into a retrieval system, or transmitted in any form, by any means (electronic, mechanical, photocopying, recording or by any information storage system) without the prior written permission of the authors and Sultan Akif, except by reviewers, who may quote brief passages in a review.

The book is available at a discount when purchased in a large quantity for your corporate and conference use. For information, please contact Two Sisters on a Mission via email at info@experienceyourlife.ca

For the latest videos and pictures, please visit www.twosistersonamission.com

To all youth who dream of making a difference, remember you have the power to change the world. Don't be afraid to do what has not been done before. It will create a path to empower millions one day.

To our parents and our mentors, thank you for empowering us. You are the wind beneath our wings.

CONTENTS

1	JOURNEY TO DRAGONS' DEN	1
2	OUR LEARNING ENVIRONMENT	13
3	THAT SOMEONE IS US	27
4	LEARNING OUR LESSONS	39
5	OFF THE BEATEN PATH	55
6	TWO SISTERS on a MISSION LAUNCH	68
7	OVERCOMING CHALLENGES	88
8	FACING THE DRAGONS	99
9	THE WIND BENEATH OUR WINGS	112
10	INSPIRATIONAL ART	134

CHAPTER 1: JOURNEY TO DRAGONS' DEN

"The world will not change with just good intentions. Lives will change, and are changing when we use our professional skills for the pursuit of human ideals. We impact lives when we take action and create sustainable social initiatives that make a real difference".

These words moved us when we first heard them from our dad, and they move us today. They inspired us to start the journey we are on right now – a journey full of adventure, fun, impact and overcoming our doubts. Through this book, we want to encourage others to embark on similar journeys of following their dreams no matter how impossible they may seem.

We are Fatima & Amna Sultan, the founders of Two Sisters on a Mission. At the age of 10 and 8, we are Canada's youngest social entrepreneurs on a mission to make a real difference. We are honored to share that at the time of publishing this book in September, 2019, we have done 40 keynote speeches around the world at major conferences and successfully competed in various business competitions. The biggest event was facing the Dragons in Dragons' Den Canada (episode will go live in fall 2019 across Canada). In addition, we have been honored to do keynote speeches at events like Microsoft DigiGirlz, Experience Your Life Expo, Toastmasters Gavel Clubs, Vaughan Social Enterprise Challenge, Share Love Celebrate event, University of Toronto Mississauga Startup event, University of Waterloo Women in STEM conference, Youth Slam by Speaker Slam, Fearless Voices, VJ TV, Social Startup Challenge, Venture Weekend Hackathon, LinkedIn Local Brampton, Rose Theatre, Milton District High School, Castlebrooke Secondary School and many others. This year we were honored to win several awards including Toastmasters Gavel Club Canada Leadership and Communication Award as well as first place award at one of the biggest speaking competitions in Canada called Youth Slam 2019 in under 18 category.

This book is actually not about any of our accomplishments as we truly believe we are two very ordinary kids. All we want through our social business, through our speeches and through this book is to drive impact. We are grounded in purpose and nothing else really matters. All our projects, including this book, have only one objective. It is to drive real change in the world by helping people connect with their power. We simply saw an opportunity to make a difference and stepped out of our comfort zone to make it happen. We are not more or less gifted than any other youth on this planet. We believe that every human has the potential to make a difference if they connect with their power, their purpose, their unique abilities and keep those people in their mind who need their help. We realized that our actions have the power to transform someone else's life. We all, each and every one of us, has the power to change lives and make a difference in the world. We hope to inspire others to follow their dreams by sharing not just our successes but also our challenges. We have so much still to learn but we have a message to share as well. A simple message that we all have the power to make a difference. We all can do what has not been done before. If it hasn't been done before then it is simply an opportunity to create a path that will empower millions one day.

We will share our story of attempting something that has not been done before, our journey, our challenges, our wins and our mentors in this book in a very real way. The only thing we hope to achieve is to inspire more people to take action, regardless of their age. To follow their own dreams no matter how crazy the dream may be. To truly believe that anything is possible if they lead with love and purpose.

So, what is our social business all about? Our passion and our social business is called Two Sisters on a Mission (www.twosistersonamission.com). Our mission is to make a real difference in this world, and we want to bring the world together through art and positive energy. We want to inspire people to follow their dreams. It is an online art store on which anyone in the world can buy an original painting, a small or large print, or custom sized print orders for their workplace, home or event. What sets our business apart is that each artist is carefully selected for their message and positive energy. We get the artists, their art, their story and their struggles and bring it to life. Along with the art, the customer engages with the story of the artist and their inspiration for the masterpiece. These are artists whose art has never left their immediate surroundings and very few people know about them. Now, those prints are going around the world through our social business and we want to light up every boardroom, office space, living room and events with positive energy through the incredible messages captured in these paintings. At the moment, the business is successfully supporting multiple artists from around the world.

Let's take a step back and start from the beginning. We were building a library with our parents as part of our family's objective of building 100 libraries all around the world (www.libraryinaweek.com). We are all-in as a family to make a real difference. Our dad was born in extreme poverty and survived on less that 50 dollars a month for years. Books changed his life and he became a global technology executive but left that career to make a difference in the lives of youths. As of right now, he has built 32 libraries in 9 countries with his own hands and local volunteers. We have been with our parents on many builds working shoulder to shoulder with other kids from the local communities.

There was a specific moment in these builds that inspired us to take action and create Two Sisters on a Mission. We were building a library in a First Nations community in Canada 2500 km away from our home and we met a first nation artist by the name of Jason. He showed us his art and what it meant to him. His art really moved us as it was incredible. In a moment of clarity, we saw an opportunity to take action, to bring that message to life for the world to witness. His story and his art can be a life changer to many and transform the way people look at life. Stories like his are meant to be known. That is when we knew that we needed to bring his message of respect, love and self-belief to the world. The world will be better with that message surrounding more people.

That's how it all started. From that point onwards, we have built everything ourselves, including designing our logo, building our website and creating our business cards. When you will see our logo, you will see our personalities are reflected in it. Amna is in the green and she is all over the place and Fatima is the focused one. This may surprise you but Two Sisters on a Mission is our second business. The first one was a complete failure and we will write about it in this book. We learned the valuable lesson that if you want to change the world, you need a good business model and a great product built on purpose. Failure is part of the journey and it always teaches you a lot. Fear of failure should never hold someone back from trying something that has never been done before. As you can imagine, we encountered every obstacle from designing our website, creating a brand, developing marketing funnels, learning big words and even bigger concepts. At the end of the day we believed in bringing the stories of our artist to life as they needed our help. It was with that belief that we were able to create something that has been winning awards across Canada.

We find our power from the artists and they are just like family to us. When we are about to take on a big stage there is obviously some nervousness. That is when we remember who we are speaking for and who is with us in spirit. When we speak or write, we are not alone. We speak for Jason, who paints in a first nations reserve and brings the culture to life. We speak for Daviel who paints for the blind. We speak for Yasmani who paints in his bathroom because that is the only well-lit room in his house. We speak for Boon Choo who paints with one hand and walks with a limp. We speak for all the boys and girls, for our artists, for everyone who is trying to follow their dreams but are told over and over again that somehow maybe they are not enough, because they don't have this or they don't have that. Well our message is simple, anything is possible, and we all are enough! We all have everything that we need to be successful and all we have to do is start following our dreams with our full potential.

We are two ordinary young girls full of dreams and taking action. We have one question for you. Have you stopped doing something due to fear? When we ask this question in our speeches, most of the hands go up. We think there is a little girl in all of us, one that is too afraid to speak up. One that is too afraid to follow her dreams. We believe that the time is now. Will you give that little girl inside of you a voice? The voice to rise. The voice to fight. The voice to go after her dreams and a voice to make those dreams a reality and the power to bulldoze every single obstacle that comes in her way. We, together, are the change the world needs. Let's not worry about how old or young we are. Let's go after our dreams and that will show this world that we are the change the world needs.

When we started this project, we had no idea how big it will become. We did not know how fundamentally it will change the course of our lives and open opportunities for us to deliver even more impact. It all seems like a dream. We have so much to learn from everyone we are meeting, and we are definitely approaching the world with the hope of coming across something new every day. Our purpose is to bring a positive change around the world. As you read this book, our only request is to keep an open mind and be ready to let your thoughts roam as you read this story. This book is not about us but the power and potential that is within everyone including you. Whether you are seven or seventy years, believe that your age doesn't decide your ability to make a difference. We truly believe that.

What holds us all back in life is often a feeling of doubt that we are not enough to drive the change we want. We had many moments of doubt in our journey too. We wanted to do so much for kids we saw in our builds but kept wondering can we make a difference. We are just two kids with no resources. We kept on seeing the relentless work of our parents to make a difference and the lives it was impacting. It was so real and we were right in the middle of it! Supported by our tribe of change makers, we slowly started to believe in ourselves and it changed everything. We found our power by seeing the impact we were having in lives of others. When we had doubts, we reminded ourselves of our purpose which is to make a real difference in the lives of our artists and it would inspire us again. Age is just a number, and anything is possible. The only thing that limits success is the boundaries created by our own mind. Our mentors helped us tremendously to develop this perspective.

This chapter would not be complete without recognizing the amazing people that have shaped our journey and have been foundational to our success. This book contains our view on the best qualities that we saw in our mentors and the way they approach life. These qualities can help everyone find their power. We got to meet a lot of amazing people, who were not just successful but more importantly they knew what to do with that success in terms of empowering others. They grow along with people around them and that's what makes them happy and more successful. This is the reason why successful and happy people do not push others down but try to lift them up by helping and encouraging them. We have dedicated an entire chapter to them in this book.

Above all, we want to recognize the thousands of people who have encouraged us as we chased our dream. We are grateful to every person who has played a role in shaping our journey and helped us make a difference. Our impact would not be possible without you. You have made us who we are, you have made this book what it is. Now as a reader you are part of the Two Sisters on a Mission tribe! You have taken action to support us and encourage us by getting this book. Our tribe's energy, passion, sincerity and support are the driving forces that help us move forward. They keep fueling us to reach more people and spread more smiles.

This is the story that started off as a dream and is slowly becoming a reality. As you turn every page of this book, you will be traveling with us to new places through our story. You will be with us as we describe when we decided to follow our dreams and you will feel our emotions when we describe the challenges we faced. We have a request for all the supporters who are reading this book. Keep an open heart, take a deep breath and let your thoughts dance. We may be younger than other social entrepreneurs, but we have big dreams and a desire to make a real difference through this book. This book describes the ups and downs that are part of the journey of any change maker, big or small. You will be able to relate to many things mentioned in this book, and we hope that this book will help you just as your support has helped us. We have written this book with our heart. It is to drive change so we can do more good in the world together.

Now let's jump into the story. There were two big projects our family has started that shaped our learning experience. As captured above, we travelled with our parents to build libraries around the world as part of Library in a Week. In addition, we also helped our parents organize one of the biggest youth employment, entrepreneurship and empowerment events in Canada (www.experienceyourlife.ca). As we went to different countries, we saw two worlds at odds with each other, where in one world everybody had the resources they needed and in the second, people were struggling for basic needs. Our young minds could not comprehend this divide and why it existed in the first place. Being a kid, we wanted the wonder woman or the power rangers to show up and save the world. Maybe they can get people to see the struggles of others. Maybe a superhero will bring them presents and save them? We wanted every house to have Dora or Diego to be their friend and give them what they need to succeed in life.

We thought about this and then realized, why are we not doing anything? We all can be someone's superhero today, or be a good friend who spreads smiles by lending a hand. We all have that power. If each one of us decides to help one person around them, soon the world will be filled with all the people who are willing to help yet there will be no one who will need it. We all have the power and the world does not need superheroes to save and help others, our world needs you and us. Our world does not need miracles to solve our problems, it needs efforts and action from you and us to solve each other's problems. Our world needs us to understand our talents, and abilities and put them to good use. Our world needs us to build sustainable businesses that make a huge difference in lives of people. If we can't change everything in this world, why not start with a single person and change their world today? It is the tiny acts of kindness that can bring about a big difference.

We realized that the world needs one thing from all of us – to act. That's exactly what we decided to do. We decided to take a big step towards opening up our project

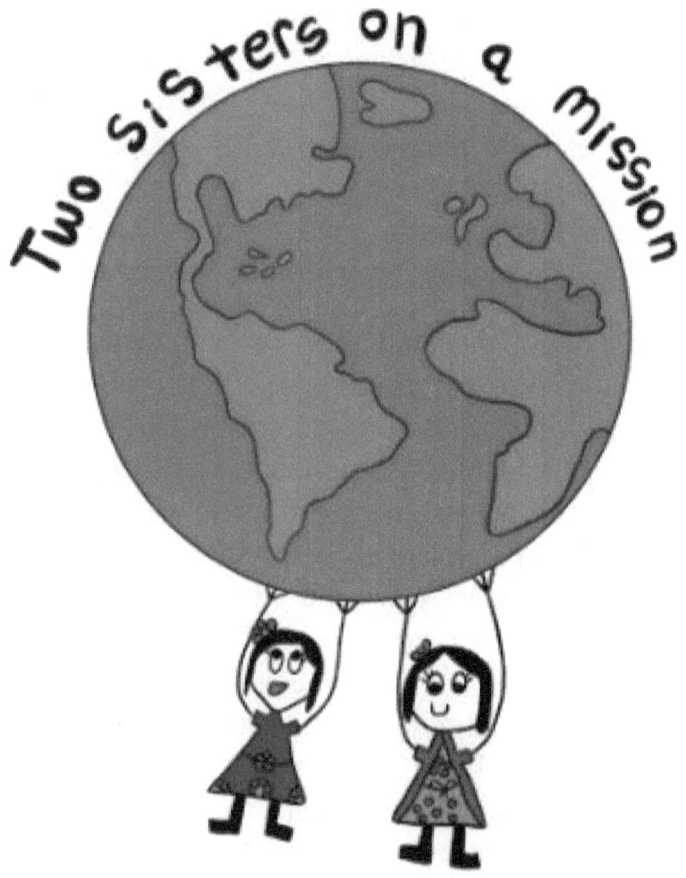

The Two Sisters on a Mission logo was so much fun to design and our personalities are reflected in it. When you meet us, you will know exactly what we mean! We drew many versions by hand and finally picked this one.

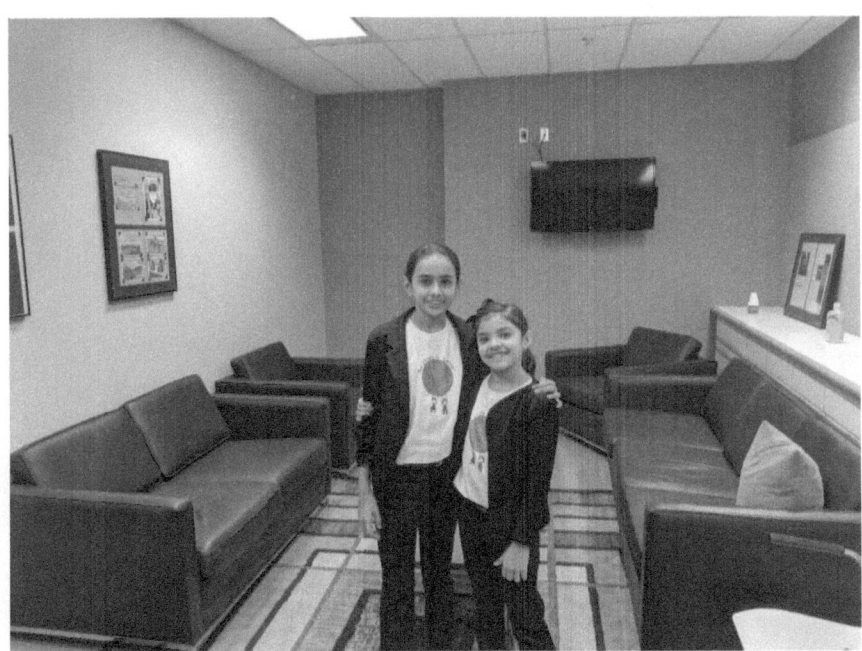

(Above) This picture was taken moments before we went in front of the Dragons at Dragons' Den. We were so excited! (Below) Our booth at University of Toronto Mississauga Startup event

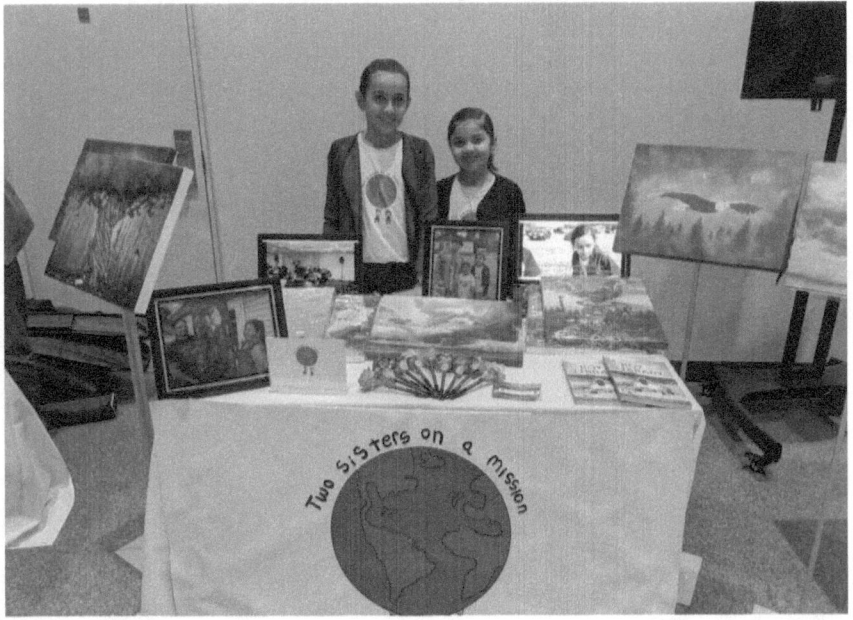

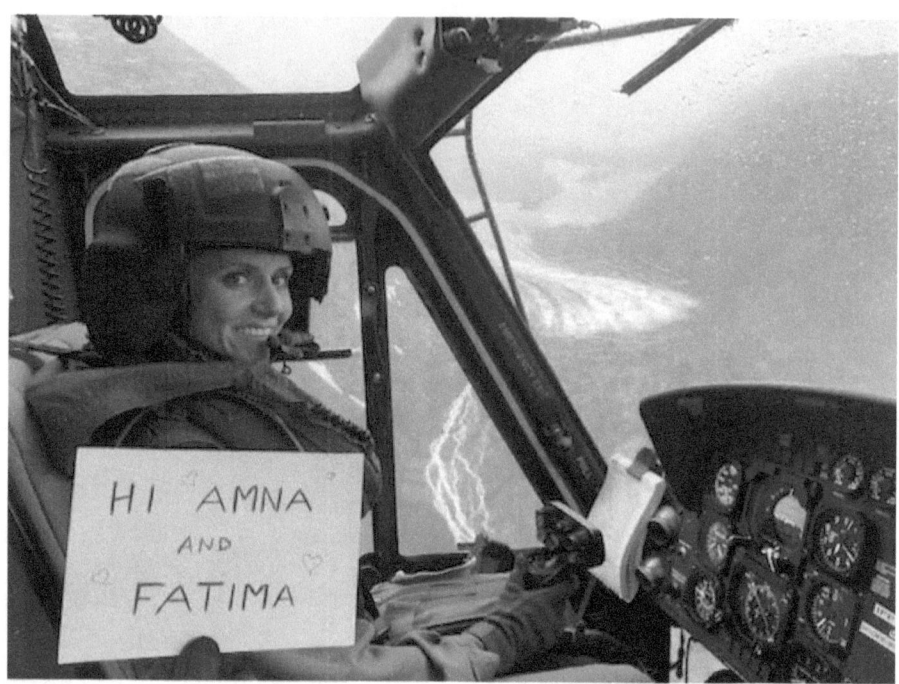

(Above) Major Alexia in her helicopter. The sign "Hi Amna and Fatima" really made our dreams fly! She is one of our biggest role models (Below left) At the Microsoft office with our mentor Karen. It was an amazing experience to present to 200 high school girls at Microsoft DigiGirlz. (Below right) At City of Vaughan Social Innovation Competition. Every other company was run by adult entrepreneurs almost three times our age. We came in the top 20% and learned so much from the experience.

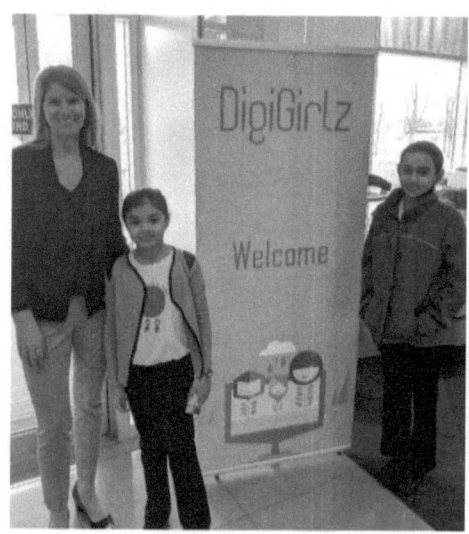
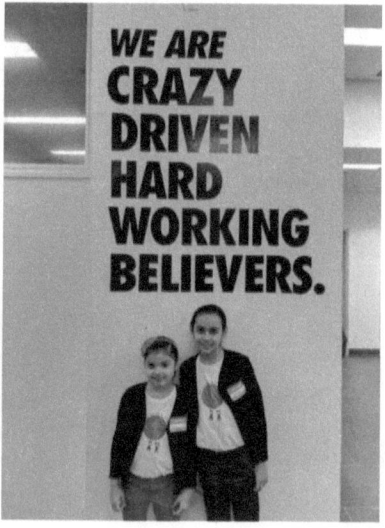

CHAPTER 2: OUR LEARNING ENVIRONMENT

There are two life experiences that have fundamentally shaped our way of thinking. One was building libraries around the world with our family and the second was being project managers at Experience Your Life Expo. In both life experiences, we learned so much. It was all part of the immersive and experiential learning curriculum that our parents had designed for us, but we never really knew it at the time. Being immersed in an environment where there was an opportunity to help others actually helped us find our power.

Helping humans unlock their potential is a passion of our dad. Prior to becoming a social entrepreneur, he was the Worldwide Solution Director for Public Sector solutions in Microsoft Services. This included education industry solutions. In this role, he got to go around the world working with the most innovative solutions and the biggest thought leaders in the field of education. He learned from the best and most important people around the world on where the future of work is going, what the world will look like and what skills we must have in the future to be successful. When he left his corporate job to follow his dream of making a difference in young lives, his passion was to provide a platform that truly empowers youth. He created Experience Your Life Expo which is now one of the biggest youth employment, entrepreneurship and empowerment events in Canada.

We were so lucky to have the opportunity to see this project come to life across five years and we got to play an active role in it. We had the title of project managers for the Expo and we were making real decisions with him. We were only 6 and 4 years old when we started to plan the event with him, always excited to see the rush of people coming on the day of the event. He believed in us even though we had no experience doing such a big task! He believed that you only get experience by doing things.

Fatima was 6 years old and Amna was 4 years old when we ran our first booth at the Expo with the support of several volunteers. Our main job on Expo day was to sell products that increase awareness of social causes. Our products ranged from Experience Your Life hats to Bracelets of Hope from little girls just like us in Vietnam. We were so excited to talk to people from all over the world and getting to know them better. In the process, we were also getting rid of our shyness little by little.

We were learning essential life skills like making a decision to change things when things are not working out as planned. For example, we were sitting on a chair behind a big table. We felt completely boxed in and separated from the rest of the Expo and we knew that if we stay behind this big table, we would not be able to make any sales at all and that means zero revenue for the causes. That meant that we would not be able to support those that needed our help. In life, there are always choices. We realized, people coming to the expo and visiting our booth were looking for jobs but people exhibiting were providing them. We were focusing on the wrong customer by being in a stationary booth! As we had been given the power to make decisions, we thought of a solution and we decided to be creative in our sales approach. We decided to walk around, with a big bag of stuff that needs to be sold to the exhibitors to grab their attention. We were successfully able to sell many things and our bag quickly started to empty.

We got support from our role models like an RCMP officer and many others! Changing our sales model was a challenging task as we had to do it on the go. Our parents supported us as they gave us the full responsibility for the task and what we didn't realize at the time that they were teaching us the life skill of 'how to make a decision' and taking ownership for the outcome. By accomplishing that simple, yet intimidating task, we felt so good. We tried many different pitches. For example, we had remembered this person selling apples in a movie so we would walk around chanting in the same tone "Get a hat for 15 or 20 dollars. Just by purchasing a hat, you can support a family in Mexico." Now looking back, we can clearly see how silly we would have looked as two little girls walking amongst federal employers, police officers, senior executives and big organizations but we didn't care at the time. As a change maker, once you care about the cause, forget about how silly you may look when trying to make it happen as your actions matter.

Maybe it wasn't the catchiest sales pitch in the world but it got the point across of what we were trying to do, why we cared, and it worked well! We were realizing that we had power, we had a voice and that voice needs to help people.

We were finding our power to make a difference without even realizing it. One year later, the Expo came again! Our memory from last year was still clear in our minds as if it had happened just the day before. As we entered the building, we asked ourselves the questions, "Who are our customers and what are their needs? This time, would it be a firefighter, a police officer, a pilot or an attendee who came to the expo? Who are the people that we will impact through our business?" After setting up our table with a nice table cover, a photo of us from last years expo, some props and things that we wanted to sell, we were all prepared for a successful day of selling. Anyone could point that out by the look of excitement on our faces. We were ready!

We had a lot of fun talking and meeting different people, as always. The shyness we had at the beginning of the previous year's expo was slowly going away. We were in our zone and everything was coming naturally. We noticed something. We were not just selling. More than the selling part, we were talking to the people this time about all kinds of things and that was something that we were never comfortable doing previously. We were learning a life skill which terrified us before, and we couldn't be happier. Knowing people through conversation and expressing our own thoughts helped us with our confidence. Knowing that what we were doing made a difference gave us our power. We were and still are two ordinary girls who are no more or less gifted than any other child on the planet. The immersive learning experience and encouragement was giving us the confidence to find our power and not focus on our limitations.

It is something that can work with anyone. We believe any youth has the potential to learn the same lessons when they are exposed to immersive learning experiences. We believe we were not unique or special in any way, but it was the environment that was shaping our way of thinking. We were getting ready for something much bigger without even knowing about it.

The main point of the Experience Your Life Expo is to help youths connect with life changing employment opportunities. Each year, we were able to impact thousands of lives by doing just that, but our young minds were curious about a question. The students and young professionals that were attending the event were from great universities and colleges. They had amazing grades in high school to be accepted into such universities. They had followed the path, but they were in big lines waiting to get a chance at a good job. That just did not seem right to us. These were great people, smart, intelligent, much wiser than us but the opportunity seemed out of reach. Although our event is one of the best in the country, we knew there are hundreds of employment events going on around the world, and millions of youths are experiencing the same situation in their life.

It bothered us to see so many people waiting in a long queue to get an opportunity to get a job. We also noticed that many people would be applying for many very different types of jobs. We could see that getting a job as a young person is hard. We could see that many would be willing to take the first good job that comes their way. As a child, you ask the most basic questions. They had studied something for four years so why are there not enough jobs for what they studied? If they were going to work in a profession that they never studied for then what was the point of all those exams, tests and learning if it was not going to be ever applied in the real world. We could see that many were really trying hard to get a good job, but they had done everything right, so why were they in this situation? We didn't have an answer.

Although we did not have an answer, we did find the right question to ask. We asked our parents, "At what age does a person decide their career and what things influence them?". They saw an opportunity for our curiosity to be channeled in the right direction and instead of giving an easy answer and totally ignoring the question they basically said that they had no idea.

I (Fatima) had an upcoming science fair project for grade 4 and instead of doing the typical project of making the light bulb light up through a potato, I thought about trying to find an answer for this question. With Amna's help and our parents' support, I wanted to find this answer as it was related to the dreams of people. We wanted this to be a real project, not just a kid's version of it. So, we researched on how to research and came up with our plan. We were going to create a survey on Survey Monkey website and ask people this question. We will send this out to a specific group of people. They would not be the ones that were students or the ones that had not started working. These would be people who have been working for over 3 years. In other words, the answer we were going to get would be real.

I (Fatima) wanted to know the main idea behind selecting their profession, was it their dream job, or a steppingstone to a better job, a movie, a role model or was it just because that's where they were able to find employment? I wanted to find out why people end up in a line if they do everything right? Are they happy doing what they love? I also wanted to know if the work people are involved in gives them satisfaction. All these questions were revolving in the back of my head and our parents encouraged us to find the answers. I was so eager to have all these questions answered that I decided to conduct a detailed research on the very topic.

I created a simple questionnaire-based survey through which I could get a lot of answers without having to go through the very long process of interviewing large amounts of people. I sent it to my dad's network of people who have been working three years or more to fill this out. I figured it was important to have the three-year requirement to get the right information.

So, after all these decisions into how to get the most relevant results for my survey, I sent this out and got 63 responses. When the results charts were created on Survey Monkey, I was shocked. It was very surprising to see so many people who are not satisfied with the job they do. They did not seem to enjoy it.

The other surprise was how people find the profession that they end up doing. I had the following question in the survey, "what factors influenced you to choose the profession you are in right now?". I thought I could find how they plan and prepare themselves for the jobs they are doing; what drives them to join a firm, industry or a sector. I wanted to determine the driving force that influences the decision to adopt or avoid a certain profession. 57% of people responded that the profession they are in is by chance! They tried to find a job in their preferred area but were unable to do so and an opportunity came by which they took. They followed the opportunities they got in the market and whatever they got, they pursued it. The lesson I was learning is that if we follow the path, it doesn't guarantee us happiness or impact. Then why follow it? Why not do something different that is aligned with our dreams? What is holding us back? These were all questions with no answers, but I knew I was asking the right questions and my parents encouraged me to continue exploring.

The second shocking result was to the question, "At what age did you first think about the career you are in right now?" The average answer was 24 years old. So, most select their profession AFTER their university or college education. Most don't end up working in the field for which they go to university. I could see why my dad had created Experience Your Life so people could really get empowering job opportunities at time of change in their life. It was all coming into place.

The last question was the most important question of the whole survey and it was again surprising for us. The question was "Are you happy with the profession you are in?" The result was 43% of people said, "No, they do not like the profession they are in." It is like going 8 o'clock in the morning and coming back at 6 o'clock in the afternoon but doing things that are not their passion. These are talented people who work really hard, so the problem was not the effort or skill. We were seeing that if we all follow the path it leads to a big line. There must be a better way. My science project results were at the end of the day were based on few responses. Almost a year later, we found out that Statistics Canada had done a similar research and the trends we found were validated by that report as well. This was a real problem. Through an immersive learning environment, we were learning real skills.

We also had the opportunity to meet some truly amazing role model at the Expo and learn from them. One of them was a person named Major Alexia, who was the commanding officer of the 417 Squadron of Royal Canadian Air Force. We also met the Commanding Officer of 'O' Division of the RCMP and she really inspired us. We met so many amazing role models like Rob Van Der Ende, Karen Truyens, Khalil Alfar, Dr. Mike and Dr. Ulrich that we talk about in a later chapter. We were seeing that the world is also full of people who made their own path in life and as a result they got to pave it for other generations to follow.

These professionals think, plan and organize ways to make a difference while fulfilling their responsibilities. These role models tend to challenge the way things are and make big changes not just for themselves but for others as well. They are not afraid of taking big decisions and initiatives. They are usually flexible and adaptive to change. They see this world as a beautiful place to live in and cherish their careers, life and impact. They believe anything is possible and that mindset was starting to help us see past our limitations. We were being inspired by these role models.

Our other major life lesson came from our travels with our family to build libraries. We are not a rich family and my dad proudly drives a truck that is now approaching almost 400,000 km and always breaks down! We live within our means and we put everything we can towards self-funding our libraries. We use our resources towards these causes and in return we get an incredible impact and life experiences that no new car will ever be able to provide. We have been fortunate enough to travel to remote First Nation Reserves in Canada, towns in Dominican Republic, suburbs in Mexico and several other places. These travels were part of our immersive learning curriculum.

On one hand, we were seeing kids our age with phones, latest gadgets and every toy they could ever ask for. Their parents had worked hard to provide that for them. However, many times, we would see that the kids would often complain about how the phone was an older version or the fact that the latest toy was not purchased for them. If that is all that we ever saw, we may have felt the same way. We could see many adults complain about their car or something else that looks perfectly functional just because it wasn't the latest.

On the other hand, we were seeing a different world. We love to travel with purpose! We have always wanted to explore new places but also find ways as a family to contribute to the place. Seeing something that you have never seen before and leave something amazing behind is a feeling we can't describe. It can really put things in perspective. Little did we know, the library projects were leaving a big mark on our lives. For example, our trip to Dominican Republic and Mexico was deeply moving for us.

We saw many kids just like us, but they didn't have many of the opportunities we had been lucky enough to have. At that point, we didn't know how to react or what to do. We only saw the problems and didn't even imagine that we were capable of doing something about it? We were just kids, what could we do? All we knew was that we wanted to put a smile on faces of our new friends. We were touched by how kind they were towards us and that made us very happy. The fact they could be so full of joy even though they were living a rougher life than we had ever had to live. It was right at that moment that we found out one important aspect about ourselves. We always felt happiest when we do something that makes another person happy.

While building libraries, we would hang out with a lot of kids our age. We realized that many had to even work in houses of other people to clean after they got home from school. School was their chance to escape that life. What we did notice though was the fact that they complained less about everything and were so grateful when they got something. We played together with sticks and stones we found on the ground – yes – the sticks and stones were of the latest version! No one cared about any versions but having fun. We were learning a valuable lesson without knowing that happiness has nothing to do with what you can afford, or the latest version of something you can buy but rather in enjoying yourself with what you have. Everyone is happy when they do what they love. We were learning valuable lessons and we did not even know it.

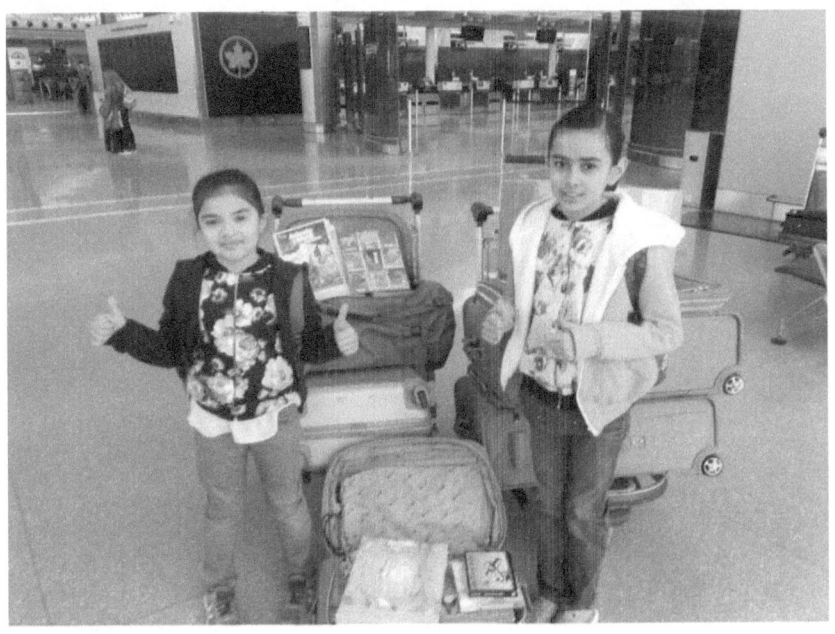

Leaving for Mexico to build our library with our family.

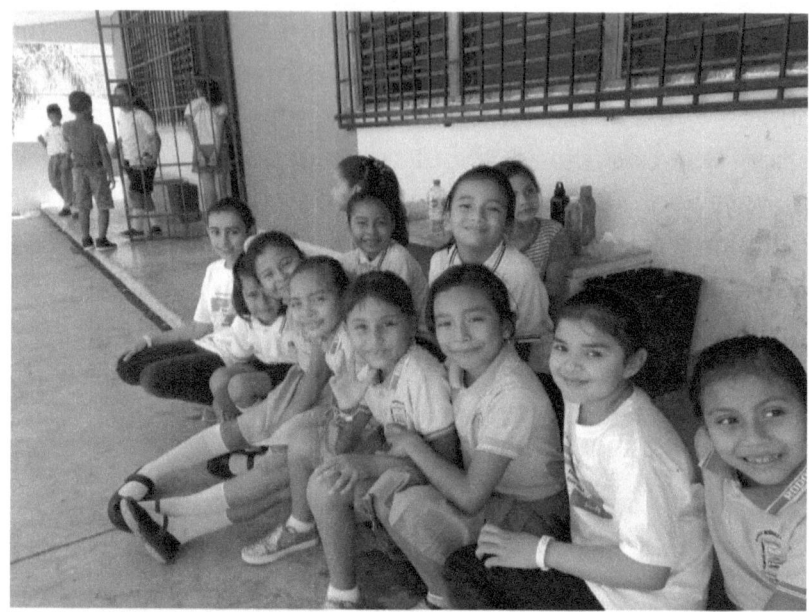

The kids we met and worked with were so amazing. This is us hanging out with our new friends

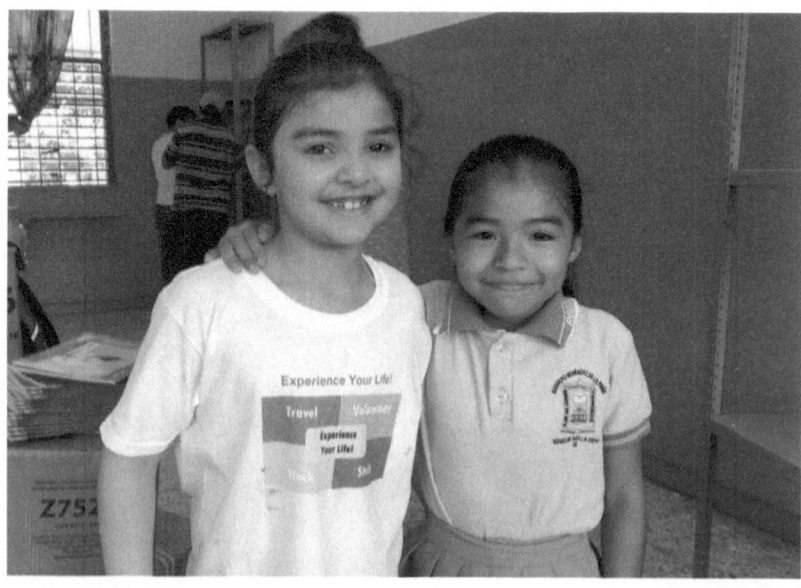

Even though we did not share a common language, we had no trouble becoming friends. This was one of the best experiences of our lives.

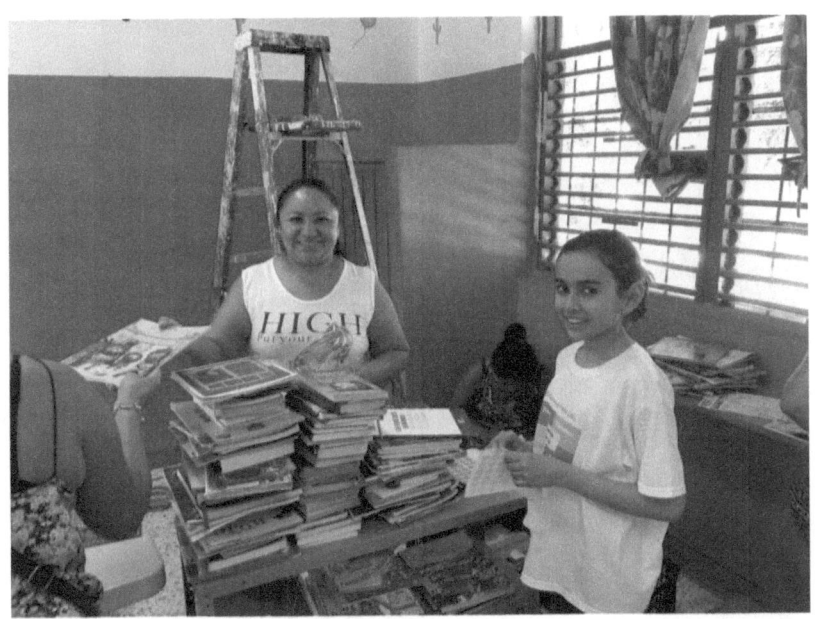

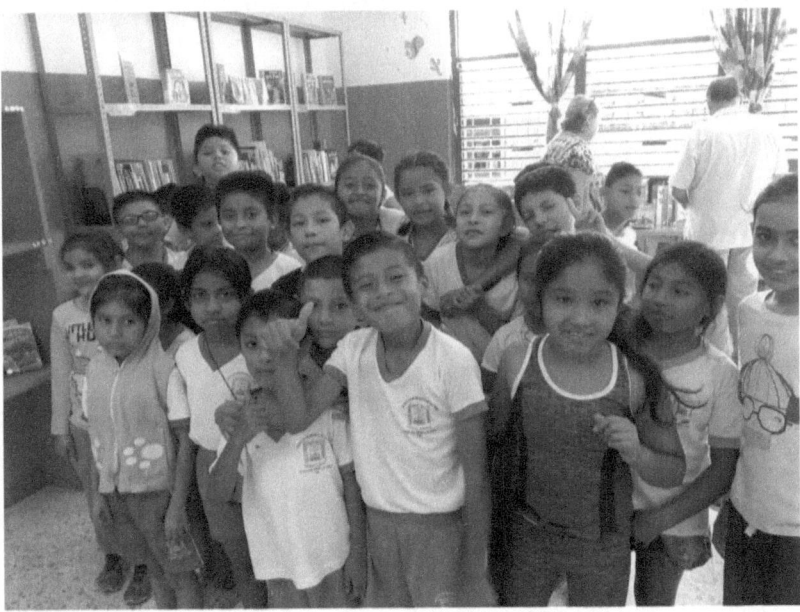

We learned so much from our new friends on how to be happy and make every day count.

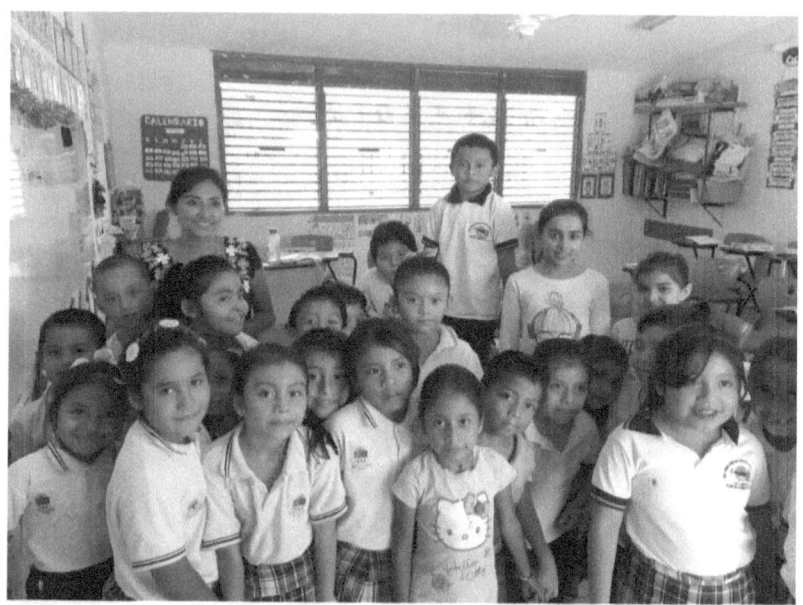

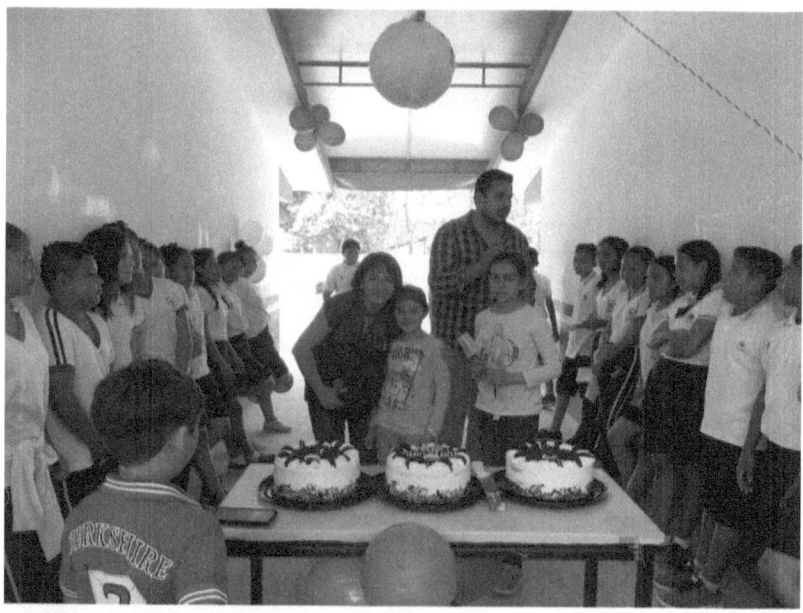

We were treated like family by those we met during the library builds. The school above has a very special place in our hearts. They organized a big party and we were greeted with so much love and kindness.

CHAPTER 3: THAT SOMEONE IS US

Visiting Dominican Republic was one of the best experiences of our lives! Just like any other kid, we were very excited about being on a plane. While we were boarding the flight, all we kept thinking about was the things we could do in Dominican Republic. We couldn't stop talking about how wonderful the journey was going to be. We annoyed our mom for some part of the trip and the other part was spent sleeping. So practically, either we slept or kept talking about our visit to a new place that we had never been to before.

When we looked out of the window, we realize that the island was covered in a tropical forest and we couldn't wait for the adventure. Our minds were thinking about the fun we were going to have, and our hearts were bouncing with joy. We started the trip just like any other family taking a vacation and stayed in the hotel for a few days. The hotel was a beautiful place to stay in. The greenery that we saw during the landing was even better on the ground.

After we settled down in our hotel, our dad rented a car for us to drive around the place. We started on our car ride and explored the countryside. As we went deeper into the country and away from the tourist places, we could see real poverty. We were too young to understand how tough the lives of some of the kids we were seeing on the side of the street really was. We had loaded the car with gifts and toys for the kids on the countryside, and when the children received them, they were so excited. We could feel their energy and their gratitude, but we did not fully understand what was happening – we just knew we were experiencing something amazing. Before those thoughts could occupy our minds, we came across a random shop. We could see bright colors inside and just had to explore.

We entered the shop and met a painter named Alberto. He was kind and very positive. His shop was small but you could feel the positive energy. The reason we wanted to go to his shop was that it held art and we love everything related to arts. Who can turn around and leave when art is on the walls inviting you to experience something new?

We knew we could learn a lot from this man in the countryside of the Dominican Republic. When we were spending some time in his shop, we heard the sound of something strange from behind the walls. We looked around to see where the strange noise was coming from. His art store had only one room that we could see but we realized it was carefully divided by the paintings and there was another small room connected to this one. That was when we discovered Alberto's small space was also his house and his garage with a scooter in it. His children were playing, and that explained the reason behind the noise. His entire life and possessions were, literally, right in front of our eyes. He lived with his two little children and a beautiful wife. They didn't have much but they were happy!

Alberto has a single scooter to travel with his family. Many people choose the best car for their family while Alberto has no choice but to use the small scooter for a family of four. He was one of the lucky ones that had a scooter while many other simply had to walk and could not leave their immediate area.

People are sometimes not happy with their house even when they have a garage with two or three vehicles, two spacious bedrooms, living room, kitchen, a play area, and a dining area. And yet, Alberto was content with his two rooms. He was happy that his family had a roof to stay under. Every time we looked at him, we could see this huge smile on his face. Alberto was content and happy person to be around.

His art was so amazing that we couldn't take our eyes off the paintings. It was like the colors were dancing around us while we happily watched them do so. Alberto told us that he opened the shop to support his family. He loved art, and it has now proven to be an advantage to feed his family. He was kind enough to gift us with two small art pieces. We insisted on paying him, but he did not accept. It is often those that have very little that are willing to give you everything they have.

Our parents are socially minded, and the conversation went deep very quickly with Alberto. He survived on a few hundred dollars a month but that income was unpredictable. He explained that 99% of the tourists do not leave the resorts away from his city or only leave it in escorted tours. In order to sell his art, he has to go on the 'vendor day' at the resort. He has to pay USD 200 to go there whether he sells any paintings or not. He has no choice as no tourist venture into his shop like we did. Something in the way he explained his situation was very moving for us. His art was incredible yet his opportunities were very limited as there was no business that was willing to give him a shot. A seed was getting planted in our young minds that would grow years later and we didn't even realize it.

Then we told ourselves, someone has to help him. Someone out there has to put a genuine smile on his face. It takes a lot of courage and hard work to fight the challenges that come with poverty. Alberto was doing exactly that. He was also sending his two young kids to school and the home portion of his space with filled with certificates of how well they are doing in school It was so moving. If someone had the power to change his life, they should change it immediately. Though he is smiling you could see that he had a tough life. But what could we do? We wished for the best to happen to him and ask God to bless his family with good health and happiness. He was giving us so much, yet we had little to offer him. He represented so many people we met in that trip, who are fighting for their families and a better life everyday. Many are fighting for simply respectful employment and happiness. Time passed by, but the thoughts of Alberto and his family never left us. We just couldn't understand why someone was not helping him.

Another moving moment which made us reflect happened when we were building a library in Mexico. We cannot tell you how much fun we had painting the walls and adding books into the shelves. This might surprise you, but the school we built the library in was 25 years old and many of the teachers had been there for that long. We worked shoulder to shoulder with them and it was an amazing feeling. We had met a lot of nice people there and we learned one thing or the other from each one of them. The school found out it was my father's birthday. On that day, everyone was acting so strange. We knew they were hiding something from us. They asked us to close our eyes, and we did what they told us to do. When they finally let us open our eyes, they all screamed Happy Birthday together! They were extremely kind and threw a surprise birthday party for my dad. We were not expecting it.

Then they took us to the main hall outside the building. Three huge cakes and a big piñata were waiting for us! They also bought lots of pastries and juices to bring in the party mood. There was a radio to pump out some music. We were so overwhelmed and couldn't resist thanking them for their efforts. We initially played a little bit of soccer before coming back to cut the cake. The cake was distributed to all the kids who were so happy. It was so pleasant to see so much positivity in the air.

The principal of the school sang a song and urged us to do the same. We sang the song "You Raise Me Up" and laughed like there was no tomorrow. Then came the time to smash the piñata! We all gave it a try. We all took turns trying to crack it until one of our Mexican friends did exactly that. Then came the tsunami of candies from the Piñata. Who doesn't love that?

They gave our dad so many greeting cards with beautiful words. The love was so real and we felt like we got ourselves an extended family. The students told us that they were planning to go on a field trip that day but dropped the plan to celebrate with us. They wanted to spend time with us and share our happiness. We will always cherish the love they showered upon us that day. We could see that even with very limited resources, they gave us so much, but many lived in hardship. Why wasn't someone helping these youths?

What we didn't realize is that through this immersive learning experience, we were learning valuable lessons. We were seeing how people come together when the intentions are positive and pure. How we were all really the same at the end of the day. That day the students and staff gave us so much more than anything we could have done for them.

During the visit to the schools we got to meet a lot of students. We told a lot of stories to the little boys and girls who attended the school and they shared their stories with us. We saw so many kids who were just like us, but many lived in hardship. The thought popped up again – Why wasn't someone helping them? Over time, we made many new friends. They were all very friendly and courteous to us. Then again, we told ourselves, someone out there must have the power to make a difference in their lives. Someone should take action and start helping these families.

It's sad that some people use their power and wealth for their own benefit and not to help others. It's surprising that some families don't even have 8 dollars to feed themselves whereas we see children our age sometimes flash their $800 worth phones. You can invest 800 dollars for entertainment and still be unhappy. Some families work the whole day to get at least 8 dollars to feed their empty stomachs and still be happy. We don't need more people who sympathize with this, we need more people to take action. To build social initiatives that drive real change. We still were not sure how to process what we were seeing but we knew we had to do something at that moment.

Sometimes, just the small things can bring a broad smile on someone else's face. We will give you one example. When we were studying in a hotel lobby while backpacking in the Caribbean, we noticed a family sitting next to us, planning to leave the hotel in a few hours. Then the father bought a lot of goodies like chips, biscuits, and cookies. We started to wonder what they were going to do with so much food. It was just the mother, father, and a teenage daughter. They sat there, smiling and talking to each other while the food rested beside them.

What took us by surprise was what they did next. A few minutes later, they invited some of the hotel workers. The workers were as confused as we were but delighted when the family handed over the goodies to them one after the other. They were so happy and that brought a smile on to our faces, and you could see that family was really happy too. The workers shared their goodies with the ones who did not get them. Those workers knew how to share their happiness with someone who didn't have what they had.

When we carefully observed, we noticed that teenager was a child with special needs. She could not walk properly and needed someone to be by her side. She was also smaller than the average teenager of her age. That moment moved us. It made us question ourselves. If someone who has the challenges that she was facing can come forward to help others, why can't the others put in the same efforts? The teenager did not think of herself as a weak person. She was not weak in fact she was really strong as she used her strength to make someone else happy instead of crushing them for having something that they did not. These small things can make a real difference. Why do we wait for a big explosion to bring in the light when we can light up candles around us to achieve the same outcome?

There are good people doing good things every day and it is

inspiring. Even a tiny matchstick is enough to light a candle and that candle spreads light all around the place. That is the power of the small things you do that make a big difference. You start with something little and it goes on to create something bigger and better.

We did see the two sides of this world. They were so different and yet existed on the same planet. One side is where the people are worried about not getting their hands on the newest phone or the latest computer. The other side has the folks that worry about not getting a proper meal for the day and are still happy.

We were inspired by the school children who put a smile on my dad's face. We were inspired by the teenager who put a smile on the worker's faces. We were inspired by Alberto who smiles to see others smile. We were inspired by people who walk into a room and transform it into a happy place immediately.

Across the two worlds that we saw, we kept on wondering. Why isn't someone helping these people? Why is someone not doing something or creating social initiatives that help people? Why isn't someone taking action to bring more joy to the lives of some people that are surviving on very little. Then it hit us like a hard tornado. We got out answer in a moment of clarity.

That someone is US. That someone is YOU.

While we talked about people sitting without helping these innocent souls, were we not doing the same thing? Everyone out there is waiting for someone else to be the change that the world needs. They want a another person to be a difference that changes everything wrong in the world. Why can't we all be the change that the world needs? We started to realize that we all had the power and it was a matter of taking action. Every change in the world has started with an idea and we knew we were on to something. Then we started to connect with our power. We started to imagine a world where everyone took action and we knew we had a role to play in making that happen.

You might not know how powerful you are until you start taking action and start believing in yourself. We wanted to make a difference in the world. We were not sure what to do next but knew we had to start. That is when this story took a turn and the idea of our social entrepreneurship started to emerge. We saw something that we simply could not walk away from.

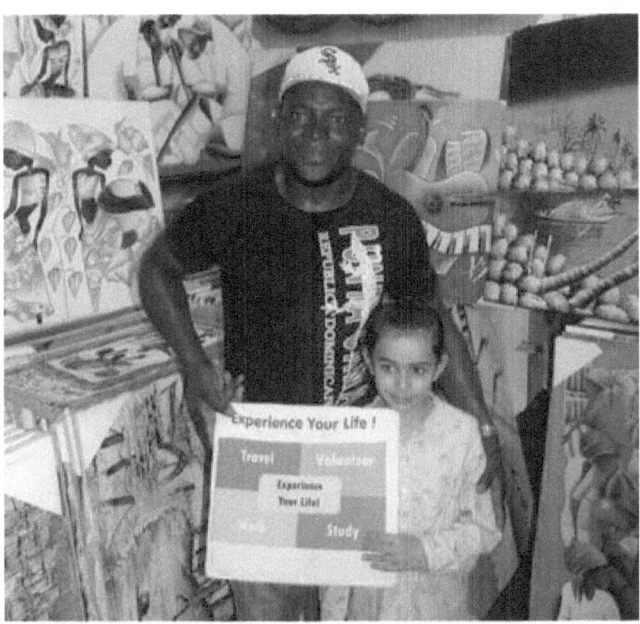

Alberto, an artist from Dominican Republic with his amazing art

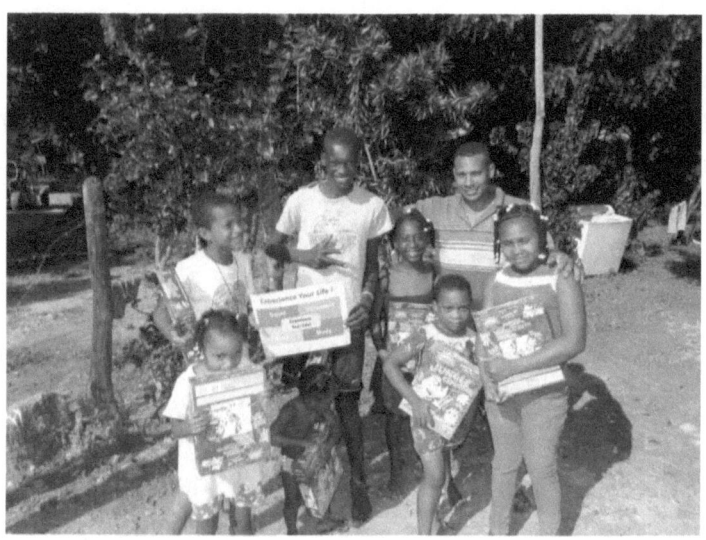

The art sets we distributed in the countryside of Dominican Republic were our favorite. The children had big smiles and appreciated it!

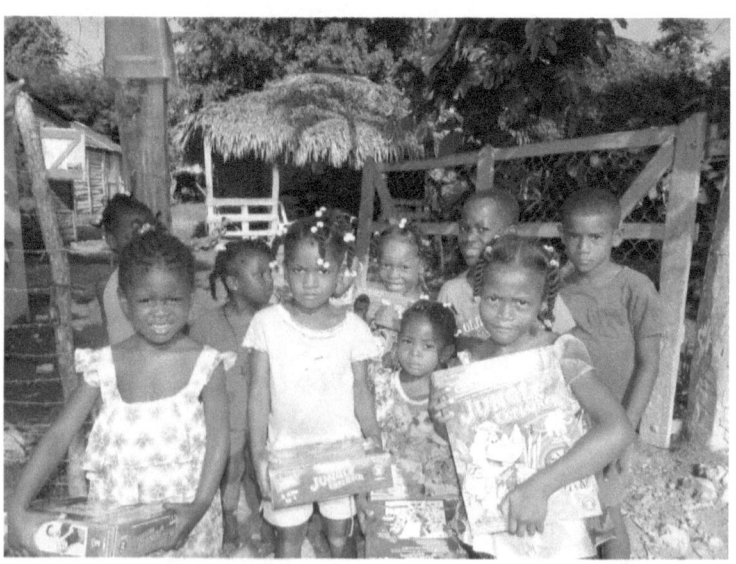

Some of the friends we met in Dominican Republic.

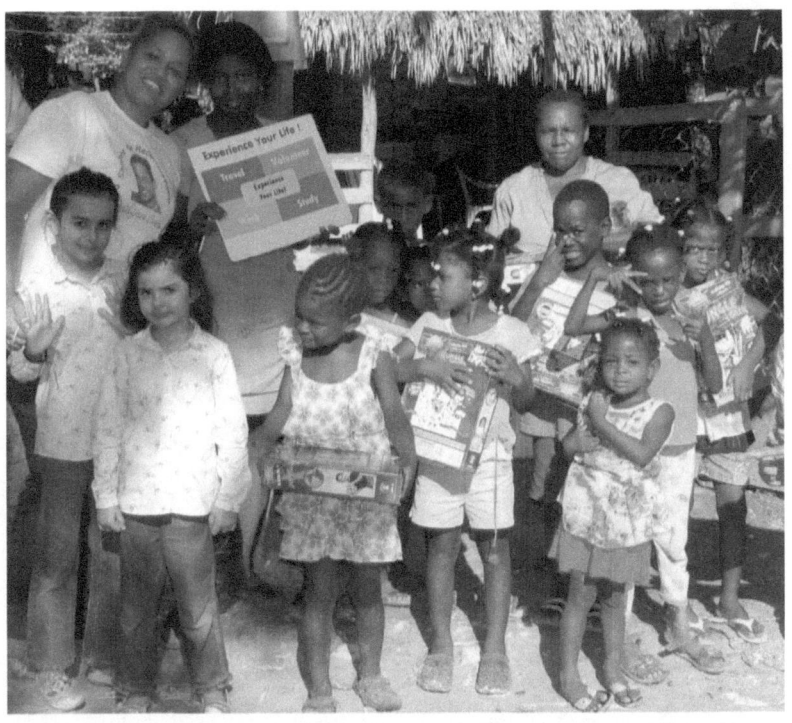

We were invited to their farm and enjoyed a delicious lunch with them

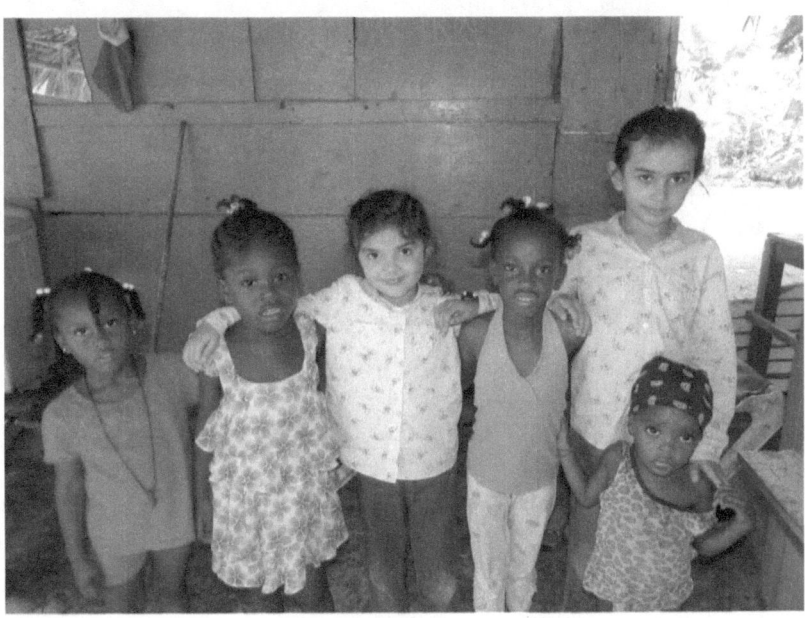

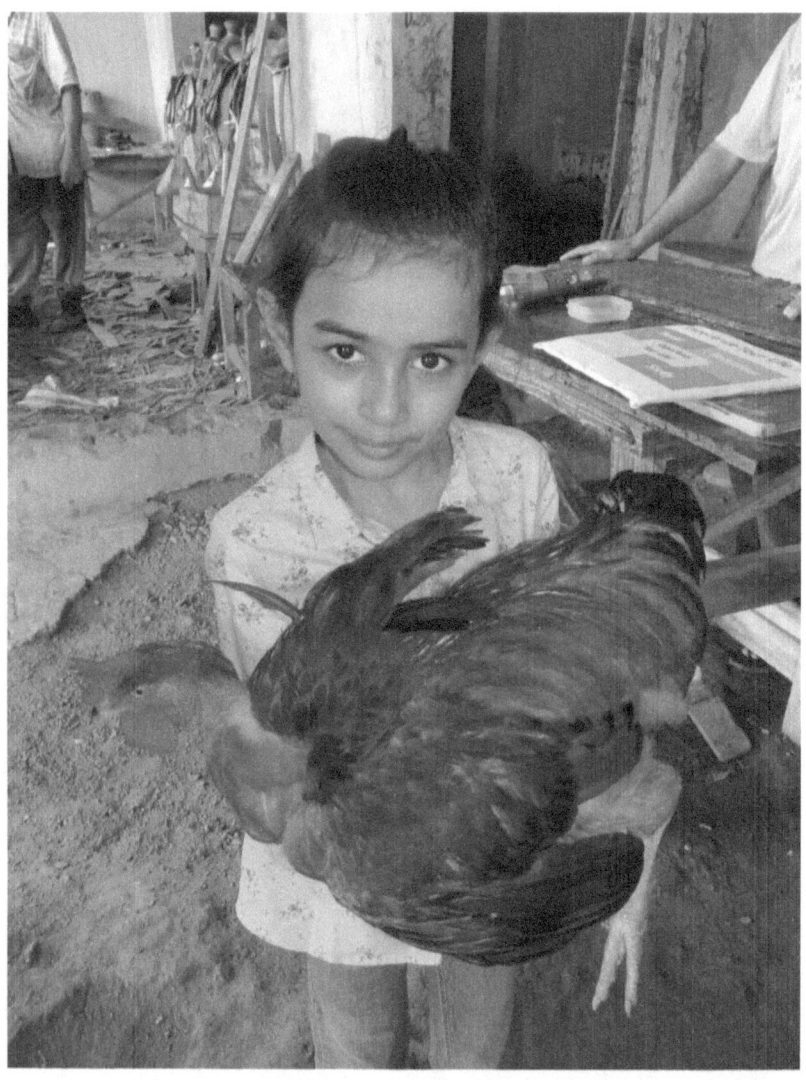

This was the first time Fatima held a chicken! Immersive learning was not just about books but about life experiences and having fun!

CHAPTER 4: LEARNING OUR LESSONS

As you read earlier, we were too little project managers for one of the largest youth employment and empowerment events in Canada with very real decision making power. Our immersive learning environments were designed so we could have fun but still find our power to make a difference.

We saw how a social business can make a real difference and we decided to setup a social business of our own. We called it "Pens for Libraries." As we all know that every small or big business comes with an idea. Now, we will tell you the story of how it all started and what we learned from it. We went as a family to build a library in Mexico. We met a woman there who worked with us to build the library. She gifted our father with a beautiful flower. We realized when we held it that it was actually a pen! The petals could move up and down. The pen was really lovely. She made it so beautifully we couldn't even believe it was a pen. The reason she gave us a gift was to thank us for building the library in her daughter's school.

Making someone feel special is the best feeling ever. It tells the receiver that we were thinking about them. While it feels good to be on the receiving end, there's a feeling of happiness when we are the one who is doing the giving. This can't be measured by money. In that moment we were both experiencing this joy, she was happy that we loved her gift. She gave us something that meant a lot to her just as the gift of the library we gave to the school meant a lot to us.

We asked the name of the shop where she got such a lovely pen and she replied, "I made it!" She then shared a story about the tragic incident in her life. She said she used to teach arts in kindergarten. Sadly, after she lost a small amount of strength in her arms and hands, she got fired from that organization. With a heavy heart, she decided to do different jobs like cleaning to make a living. She makes pens as a part of her hobby. When we heard this story, we were quite emotional and knew we had to help her.

We decided to jump right into it, and we started a business at the age of nine and seven. We purchased 500 flower pens and got to work. Our first step was to put up a page on www.libraryinaweek.com with the new product. After a launch that didn't really have much thought put into it about our target customers and their needs. We waited patiently for the orders to come through.

Then one day, a notification came on our dad's phone as were having a meal. We opened it up and read the good news, it was an order of six pens. We were very excited about the order. The whole week no other orders came. We were wondering why no-one was buying a single pen as it was only 15 dollars. At that time when we were launching the business, we didn't care about the price of the pen, we did not do any market research, we did not do any competitor research and did not even make a business canvas. We simply wanted to help the woman. The price seemed fair to our young minds based on how much we were getting it for and our margin to cover the overhead costs. We were not considering the value for the customer and the other options they have available to them.

Now that the order came, we started to really work the numbers for shipping. The shipping in Canada for a small package of that size was around 12 dollars! The price was going to be the same if you send a single pen or a pack of six. So if a customer was to buy a single pen for 15 dollars, then the customer would end up spending 27 dollars for something they can easily buy for a few dollars somewhere else.

There was another real problem with the business – the product was not of a high quality when it came to functionality. The pen was a simple pen you can get from a dollar store, the value was indeed in the art that was made on top of the pen but from a pure feature standpoint, it lacked quality. At the price-point, senior professionals would be our target market but they obviously could not take a pen to a meeting that may slightly smudge the paper as some did. Our business was getting surrounded by many problems slowly. Anyone could get a similar pen for 1 dollar at Dollarama. The only reason that made this pen stand out was the fact that this pen had a story behind it and they wanted to support us. We were losing the confidence in our product and in our judgement.

Then our parents sat us down and asked us what we learned. We gave them an entire list of things, feeling really bad in the process. To our surprise, they congratulated us! We simply could not believe what we were hearing. The fact that we learned so much is equivalent to an MBA and this is the type of education that would be hard to get any other way. We decided to reflect on the lessons we learned and do research on what makes a great social business.

Our first lesson was that your product quality must be exceptional – while it is true that sales is an emotional process and that is why people were still buying our pens, but we did not feel that we were giving them a product that we could stand behind. The product that the social business is built on must be of a high quality and functionality for it to really sell. We were learning that the best businesses are built on purpose but also have an exceptional product and an exceptional emotional connection.

It was a big learning experience. We started to attend sessions, watch videos and have long conversations with our parents about business models. We observed that traditional business models focus only on price advantage for their products and services. Companies build up their products, advertise them, then make sales by offering a cheaper price but that strategy no longer works.

As customers become more socially and environmentally conscious about their buying choices, sales are becoming less and less dependent on price of products and services. Instead, customers are turning their attention to the buying experience and how they feel about your company after they become customers. We had not taken any of these lesson into Pens for Libraries. We didn't realize that we were not just selling a product but a complete experience that needed to have everything in it.

Positive changes in society are making people value the social impact of their purchases on the environment and in the lives of people and ultimately that determines how they feel about the products and services. For our brand to make a real difference in the lives we wanted to change, it needed to provide a complete experience for the customer. Products are still important, but products can no longer stand alone; they must be built around an experience that makes people feel excited and motivates them to make a difference. That is the central concept to a social business that will have loyal customers and also make a real difference at the same time.

We also learned the importance of building a strong connection with customers and build a tribe that genuinely share a similar cause. If we can develop a product that solves a real social problem, has significant value to customers at a price that is reasonable – it will sell well and we can make a real difference.

Our parents asked us what we were going to do with all this business experience. Keep reflecting on the past or will we give things another shot when the time comes? The biggest lesson we took away from this was that in the world of social entrepreneurship, if you want to make a real difference, you must have a good business model based on value. You can't simply rely on donations and ask people for money to help other people. We must make businesses that are incredible, that drive real value to customers, but at the heart of the social business is the simple desire to make a difference for a real cause, such as improving the lives of people who are getting left behind in society. We felt really happy that we had learned this lesson and it will be with us for the rest of our lives. We knew that it was a small price to pay for the years of value that this simple lesson will give us and had we not tried our business; we would have never learned it!

The difference between success and failure is patience and determination. If we kept trying to create a successful social business and remained patient and determined, we knew one day we will achieve success. The only difference between those who succeed and those who don't is that keep moving forward no matter how slow the progress is. If we keep trying to have impact, we will eventually succeed.

Our first business was a failure and our last lesson from it was perhaps the most powerful one. We learned when to walk away from something so we can have the time back to build something even better. If we continued spending our energy on a business that has a weak foundation, we would not be able to do anything else and we would not be where we are today. We decided to close it down.

Through this experience, we were not just learning about social business and impact but also about the importance of life skills like teamwork, collaboration and inter-cultural respect. The best part about this learning was that it was all so much fun. We never realized that we were actually learning. For example, after a few months, we went on a trip to build another library in Mexico. We were so excited as we got on to the plane to go to Mexico. This ride was for about 4 hours and one of the longest ones we had taken so far. We landed in Mexico and we were happy when we got to see beautiful sights as the buss strolled along. The weather was hot, but we were extremely excited as we were going to build a library here along with local people.

We woke up early the next day and headed to outside the tourist areas where few people go. We had seen the tourist parts but this was very different and poverty was visible. What was also visible was the courage of amazing people who were working hard and were giving their best to make a difference in their own lives and in the lives of others around them.

We went to the school and started our project to make a wonderful library. We met the local change makers and got to work immediately by taking everything out from the car. Our first job was to paint the room with bright yellow and red colors to create an exciting environment for the students. We had to make it look clean and paint it in a professional manner hence we started slowly and painting continued for about 3 hours. The next step was to build shelves and we wanted to put our own energy in the project. Instead of buying the shelves, we built it all together with the locals to give it a more creative look. It was a fun and exciting experience to build something from scratch. Our dad and the parents of the students did the wood cutting and the major work but we were right with them helping them bring the tools and doing whatever we could to support them.

Creating the shelves across the room seemed like a complex task to us but with teamwork it got done so quickly. The wood had to be painted first and it takes almost a day to dry. The project continued with full momentum and everyone kept on trying to find things to do to add value. We did not realize that we were learning a life lesson on teamwork and leadership. No one needed to be told what to do. Everyone was eager to contribute in any way they could. The tasks in the project were carefully designed to ensure the project get done very quickly but what made it special was the energy. It was incredible and everyone was laughing. This did not seem like a work environment but rather a place where people would come to meet friends and family.

The project proceeded with full speed. People kept on moving the project forward and did not let anything stop them. For example, while the shelves were drying up, everyone started to mark books and arranged them according to their categories. After the paint dried, they started to place the books in order. We had a combination of both popup and picture books including awesome books like Harry Potter!

Once all the construction was done, we helped the moms and students place the decorations on the wall. We were tired but we were determined not to back out. All around us were people who cared deeply about their library so how could we let them down? We were learning another valuable lesson on teamwork and focusing on the end outcome. It is really important to stay focused when you start something and don't let your team down. We didn't realize but through this experience, we were learning how to work as a team. How to present our ideas with confidence but accept ideas from others too. We were also learning how similar people really are as even without a common language to share, we were communicating with each other through smiles and a bit of our broken Spanish.

Above all, through this experience, we were learning the power a good social project has to bring people together. To create a common energy filled with positivity, impact and purpose. We saw a dark room convert into an incredible place of inspiration in just under 72 hours when 200 people that were all driven pushed together. We saw how anything is possible when you lead with love and purpose.

Our lessons continued in different parts of the world as our social projects gained momentum. For example, we learned about empathy through another immersive experience. We have never known what it would be like to put ourselves in another person's shoes until we were in the Caribbean. After delivering our big expo, we decided to do something that we had never done before. We decided to go backpacking as a family in the Caribbean for two months. We were going to keep it very cheap, stay with locals and have an immersive experience. We are not a wealthy family in terms of possessions, but our parents proudly invest in life experiences. Since leaving his corporate job at Microsoft, our dad had made serious adjustments to his life including driving a really old truck that he is proud of (it is now almost 400,000 km) and our mom makes adjustments to ensure we only buy what we need. This allows us as a family to live within our means and not buy fancy things all the time so we can focus more on our impact and life experiences.

Our dad has developed his social business such that he can work from anywhere and we keep our costs down in Canada by not having fancy cars or eating out a lot. In our backpacking trip in the Caribbean, we found the perfect place to stay with a local family for less than 30 dollars a day and were able to explore so many things from there. We would walk for miles taking in the sights and sounds. The owner of the house and her family were very kind to us. She lived right beside us with her young five year old granddaughter named Sofiya. They helped us to settle in the room and told us everything we needed to know. She was so helpful and told us in detail about different places to visit and experiences in the city. It felt like a big warm welcome

Her five year old grand-daughter Sofiya was slightly younger than us. From the moment we met her, we were friends. The challenge was that we did not share a common language but that did not stop us from having fun. We decided to play games like monkey in the middle and many more that did not need a common language.

We enjoyed ourselves playing different card games and even made up some games by ourselves! Sofiya only knew

Spanish and we only knew how to speak English. The language of friendship is not words but the actual experience of having fun together. We didn't let the communication gap stop us from having fun.

Everyday Sofiya taught us new Spanish words. We won't deny, we did find it funny when we were learning Spanish for the very first time. We were having so much fun and found our new pretend professions where we play with neighborhood cats and do comedy shows.

We wondered if is she was alone or have any brother or sister as we did not see any other kids in the house? We would start playing from 8:00 am in the morning till late in the night! Sofiya developed a friendship with us and now she waited for us every morning. We started hanging out and she liked to eat food with us and sometimes she even had every meal of the day with us.

This sets the background of the life lesson on empathy that we learned. This is what happened. We had a very particular sunblock that we could only get in Canada that works well with our skin. That is the only one we could use in our trip. The bottle had a safety clip and had to be opened in a unique way. One day we came back and found half of the bottle empty. We were trying to figure out who used half of that bottle and realized it was Sofiya. We were very upset! When our parents came to know all about this matter, they tried to comfort us, and we had a discussion. They told us to put ourselves in her shoes. They said "Sofiya is looking up to you as big sisters. She has someone to play with, fight with and look up to that she didn't have before." Our parents were right that Sofiya was just trying to be our friend and do everything we were doing. We understood our parents advice. We had a few days left with her then why not spend it being like big sisters to Sofiya rather than worry about little things? We could keep the bottle higher on the shelf but being upset at Sofiya was not the right way as she was an amazing person.

We learnt two important lessons in that trip. The first was how similar we are in the world and we can make friends as long as we lead with love and positive energy even when we don't know the language. The second is empathy and caring for others helps you to see things differently.

The lesson on empathy continued as we continued in our trip. When you travel you come across people in tourist places that are trying to sell you something, they may be very persuasive and may follow you until you say no very firmly. It is easy to get angry but if you put yourself in the same shoes as that person, you will come to understand how much they struggle. For something as simple as selling our girl guides cookies we experienced the wonders of what constant rejection does to you. It drains you and constantly selling is one of the hardest things to do. Sales are hard, sales are draining and sales makes or breaks you financially. Even if the people selling tourist things come off a little strong and aggressive, they are just trying to make a living. Just a small gesture of a smile or a polite "no" can go a long way to communicate the message without spoiling your day or theirs.

There is a lot that goes on throughout their day and trying to annoy you is not their objective. Despite the grinning, sometimes forced smile, every person trying to sell a tourist a service has the same daily struggle. If they had a choice, they would not be on a side of the street trying to get our attention. They work for hours to feed their family. We must always put ourselves in another person's shoes before we judge them. At that very moment, we learned a valuable lesson about life. To treat people with respect and understand where they are coming from. At the same time, expect the respect you deserve as well. You don't have to buy what they are selling but gently saying no with a smile can help keep the interaction positive for both people.

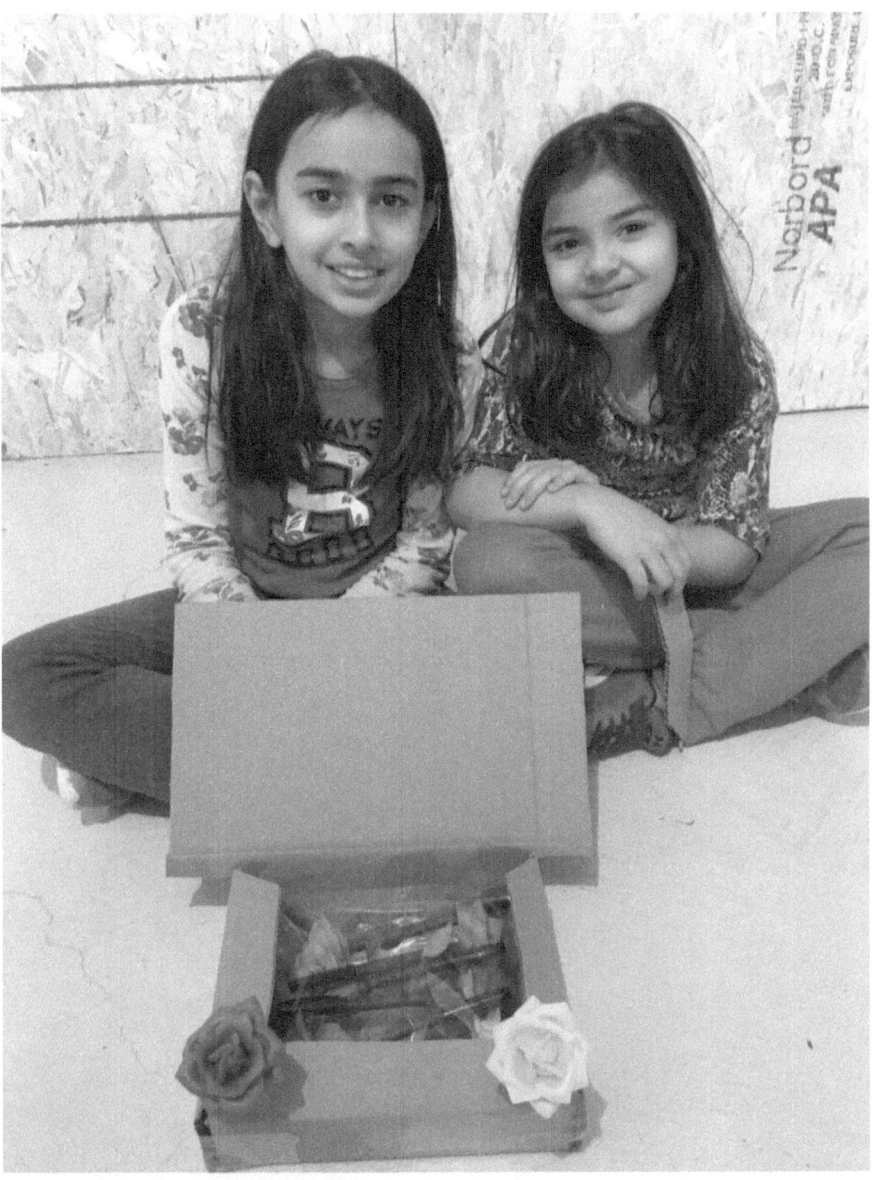

We were so excited when we got our first order, actually from someone who is now our mentor, Khalil Alfar from Microsoft! We even made a handmade custom box and sent the pens to him. The pens business never worked out but Khalil has been with us through the whole journey to this day many years later. Good mentors never leave your side.

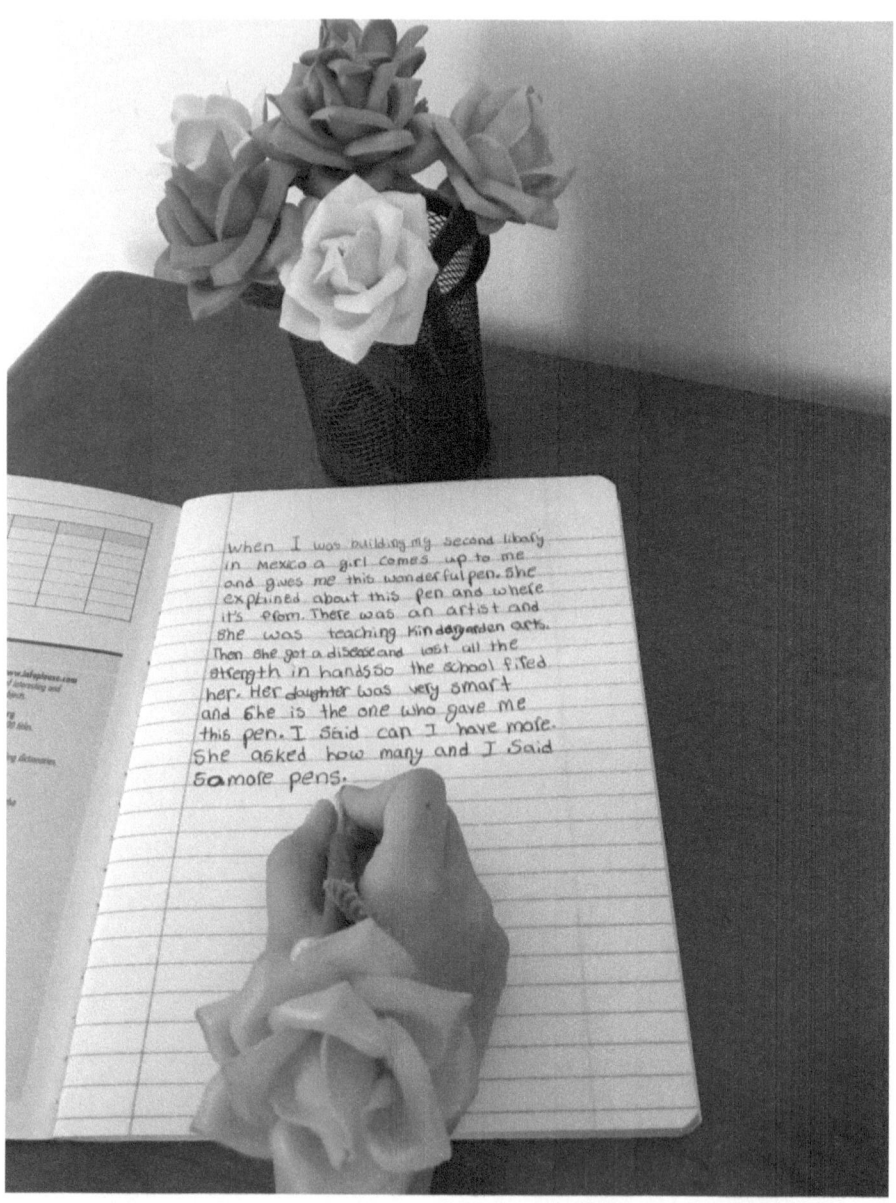

You can see why we fell in love with the pens they were beautiful but not great as a business. On a side note, we love to write. This book is a collection of things we wrote such as the one above from almost 1.5 years ago.

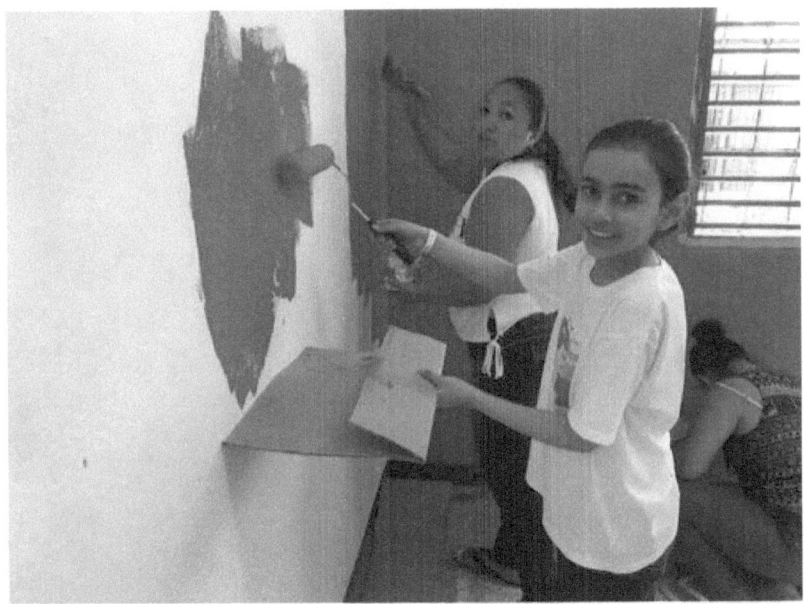

Building our library in Mexico. Painting the walls awesome but meeting new friends was even better!

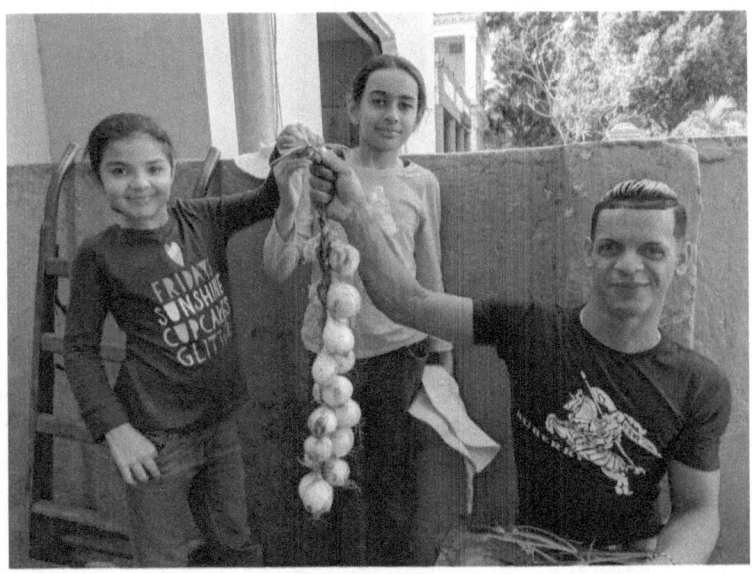

Many moments like this happened in our backpacking trip as we were living and shopping like locals. This vegetable seller taught us how to make a string of onions! People were so kind and welcoming.

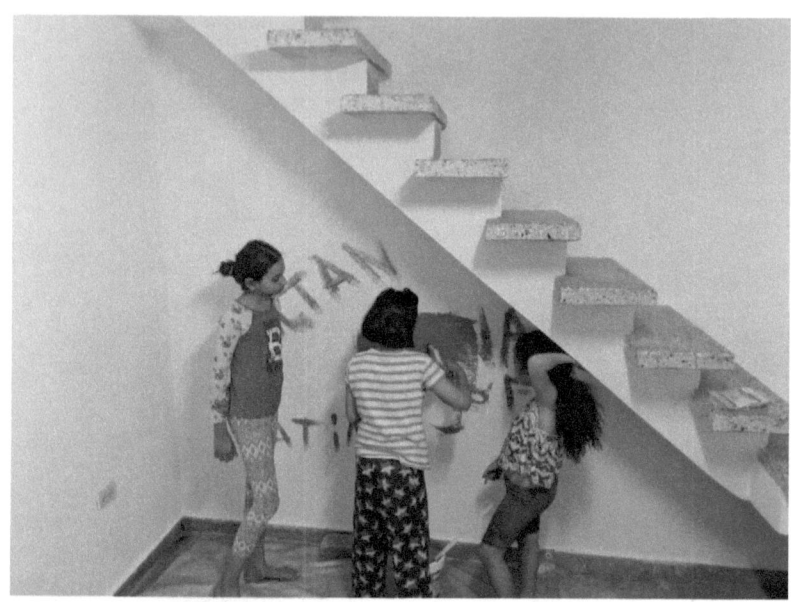

The 3 amigas – Fatima, Amna and Sofiya. We built a small play area for Sofiya to enjoy for years to come. We were writing our names on the wall so they will always be there below the paint.

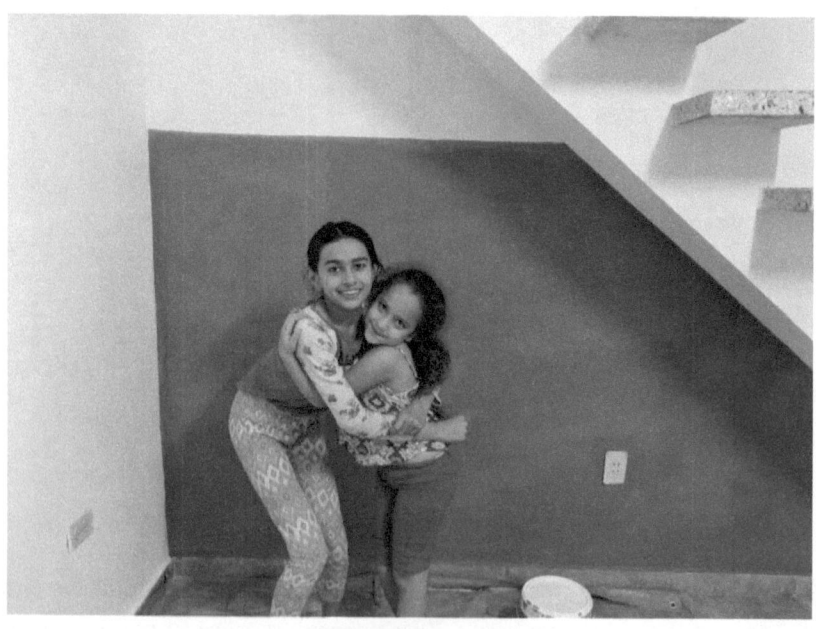

Fatima and Sofiya enjoying their friendship. No translation needed!

CHAPTER 5: OFF THE BEATEN PATH

Building a business is challenging at any age and being only 9 and 7 makes it that much harder. Add to that a social mission and the odds are really against you. That is what makes it so exciting and adventurous. While many have not built social initiatives in your youths there are a few that blazed the path such as the Keilburger brothers who built the ME to WE movement. We were always inspired by those that did not wait in the line but rather blazed a path for others to follow simply because they believed in their purpose. For them, it was all about impact and that is what inspires us.

If you love doing something then you must go for it even if the chances are low. Our mentors helped us a lot in developing this mindset simply by following their own dreams. They inspired us, guided us but let us make our own decisions and that is what was so exciting about this whole journey. They encouraged us to follow our passion even if it took us off the beaten path. On one hand, we were feeling our power to make a difference while on the other we felt a bit constrained by our routine.

We went to school from 9:00AM to 3:30PM, with 1-hour added for the commute to and from school. While 7 hours of our day was spent in school, the remaining time was consumed in completing the homework, projects, and day to day studies. School definitely had its fun moments but our experiential learning through the real world was so rewarding and the lessons stayed with us for life along with the smiles of the people we came to contact with.

We felt that if we followed the path like everyone else, we will not be able to help so many people who needed our help. We knew we had to take a different path and we believed that anything is possible. By doing everything that everyone else is doing, the outcomes are going to be more or less the same unless someone breaks free and starts doing something they deeply care about. Our mentors encourage us to connect with our power and to realize that if there was no path to our destination, then we had the power to make one. They encouraged us to choose the race and the path we wanted to run on as that determines where we end up!

It wasn't an easy job to accommodate all our activities during our normal school going routine. Every day was packed to the limit and after engaging in all the things we wanted to do, we would retire at 10 o' clock. There was no time to think about anything else as we were so busy following the path. Any work we might have managed to get done would have been of such poor quality, and we would just have to start over anyway. We knew it was better to wait until we could manage to fit the impact we wanted to have in the world into our schedule. We then thought about how long should we wait? Until middle school, but there is high school after that. So should we wait until high school, but there is university after that? Should we wait until university, but there is the big line we need to stand in to get our first job as we had seen every year at the Expo? After the first job, there is at least a few years we need to work non-stop and after that life gets even more busy. In other words, wait until we can't do it anymore! Many people who made a different in the world realized that the time to act was not tomorrow - it was today! Our dad always says that there is never a perfect time to follow your dreams but today is perfect enough to start. We were going to start and see where it takes us.

It is always our parents who inspired us to keep going, no matter how tough or impossible things seem in the moment. Our mom is our pillar of strength who encourages us to go after our dreams. Our dad had to drop out of school as his family could not afford the school fees. He survived on less than 50 dollars a month for years. He fought through life to establish himself as a global executive who has been to over 75 countries in the world. He gave that up to build libraries with his own hands. Our parents have dedicated their lives to helping others. We grew up seeing our power to do good and not our limitations. We are not a rich family but we have enough. We define our wealth in our ability to impact as many humans as we can on the planet. As a family, our objective is to change lives by connecting people with happiness and opportunities. That is what we want to continue in our lives.

There are a set of family values that we hold high and try to include in our daily lives. The values of hard work, staying purpose driven and having a great time while doing it. These are simple values, but they have given us more inspiration than any books we could have read or lectures we could have taken. It is the foundation of our entire way of living.

Our parent's guidance never failed us and we can never thank them enough for being our support system. It was like all the doubts would vanish after we think about those values.

Our parents are our role models. It is their blessings that always kept us standing tall when the obstacles were pulling us down. They taught us to stay positive and have always given us the freedom of choice to do whatever we wanted (within certain limits of course!). Everything we have learned is due to the continuous support of our parent and our mentors.

Going back to our story when were on the path like everyone else, our daily schedule was pretty hectic. Our weekends were busy too. They were packed with activities like most families and would pass by so quickly. We had no time to focus on our impact, or even the idea of a real social business. That's when we told ourselves that something needs to change so we can give the attention to our passion. We reminded ourselves that we are the change the world need. We realized we were doing a lot of things that wouldn't even help us in the long run to achieve the success or the fun that we wanted.

Finally, we decided on a good solution that was off the beaten path. We decided that the best option would be homeschooling. It didn't take us long to realize that we were more efficient. It did demand a significant amount of focus but that is also a life skill. In addition, we wanted to redefine what it means to home school. We wanted to have the time to backpack with our family, play every day with our own age group and be amongst the top in our studies by doing more than the Ontario curriculum. We believed anything is possible. We wanted to create an environment in which we get everything we hope to have from our learning experience from a fun, impact and studies standpoint. We did not want to compromise on our sleep, our education, our socialization with others in our age group or the impact we wanted to have. We got to work designing how we can achieve all of these objectives.

We understand that we were lucky to have supporting mentors and parents who saw a vision that was different to the traditional way of doing things. We were lucky that our parents trusted that we were able to handle the responsibility of homeschooling and that we had made a good decision that was best for us as students and as a person with big dreams. We were learning how to focus, how to decide, how to plan, how to perform and later realized that these are the skills identified by united nations as essential for the future world of work. We were learning how to learn from different sources of information. We were learning how to find answers and not just focus on the problem. Working with our parents, we aligned our curriculum and learning environment with the latest research and had an amazing time doing it!

You have to be strict with your studies and make sure you get everything done because you don't have teachers telling you what to do and when. On the other hand, it teaches you self-discipline. Our dad had adjusted his work so that he could work from home and we would spend a lot of time together while working on our business and studies. The traditional way was holding us back and this was an opportunity for us to open new experiences. We go into detail about how we made decisions because the bigger message in this book is to encourage others to make decisions in their lives that seem out of the path. If it works for you, go for it. Its really that simple. Soon, you will have a group of people with you doing the same.

Often what many consider as the only way is simply the path that is right in front of us. We all have the power to create our own paths as long as we are clear on what we want to achieve. For us, we wanted to make a difference, work hard and have a lot of fun doing it. We believed we had the ability to create a schedule aligned with those objectives. We created a schedule that has 5 to 6 hours of pure fun everyday with our own age group as we play squash competitively and other games recreationally. We are enrolled in several after school programs to make sure that is taken care of. Secondly, there is a lot of focus on academic excellence and we are going 25% more than the standard Ontario curriculum. We are building a business that is making a real difference. Before like most people, we were too afraid to go away from the path and go after our dreams. Once you start walking, you will make a path behind you. In our case we are walking as a family hence the path is nice and wide.

For example, our dad would go to various universities and colleges for meetings planned with senior leaders. We would tag along and study at these locations. It was so much fun to have the choice to be able to study from anywhere, from libraries to universities and colleges. From co-working spaces to after school meetups. In particular, being in universities and colleges was so much fun! For example, we went to a university one day and realized that it was the first week back from holidays for the students.

The students put up booths and gave many fun giveaways to people who stopped by for information. We walked around the many stands that were displayed but the ice cream stand was the one that caught our attention. You had to tell one exciting fact about the university to get an ice-cream and let's just say we learned a lot about the university that day! One of the professors took us to his office to discuss and exchange ideas of all sorts with our dad. It was nice to be included in the meeting with our dad and it really made us feel super special. To top it off, he offered us a slice of cake, which, of course, we gladly accepted and enjoyed. We were also invited by the head of indigenous department to join him in the office where we did a smudge ceremony. This ceremony is part of Canada's First Nations culture to clear your mind and soul from negative thoughts and focus on positive energy. It was an amazing experience.

Then we headed over to the library which is where our dad worked on his business and we completed our school studies. Once our work was completed, we joined our dad in having real conversations about the expo business. He would explain the challenges he was facing and ask for our advice. We knew it wasn't just to teach us but he valued our input and it made us really think through the problems. After that we went to the after schools' program for Squash and stayed there the entire evening! We play squash competitively and it has taught us so many things and we have so many good friends now who play the sport. Amna is currently ranked the top player in Ontario for under 9 age and Fatima is ranked in the top players in Ontario as well for under 11 age. This sport has benefitted us physically and kept us fit and healthy. We were two shy little kids and just the right environment is helping us find our power. Anyone can achieve the same results if they are exposed to the same.

We have a dream to play for Canada one day and are planning to go to US Junior Open for Squash in December.

We have a coach who believes in us and we are training for the big event these days. A good mentor can help you do something that you could not even imagine before while still creating an environment that is fun. Many Monday nights after our official squash games, most of the kids would get together in the court and play random games against one another. At times we would even use our rackets as hockey sticks and the squash ball as the puck and play rounds of floor hockey just for the fun of it. It is simply fun to play silly games with your friends and we love doing it.

One of the common challenges with home schooling is not having enough time to have fun. Well, we clearly fixed that problem as it was important for our family. In addition of a full squash schedule, we are active members of the wonderful organization called Girl Guides of Canada, which takes place on Thursdays in our area. It is a fantastic organization for girls of all ages to join. We get tasks as a troop and we have so much fun completing them. Once a Girl Guide, always a Girl Guide! It is also another place where we have made some wonderful friends and being a part of the organization allows us to become more creative as a person. Every week is different and every activity will benefit in a different way. We work on arts and crafts, share stories, and play fun games together as a group. It is an exciting way to improve creativity and have lots of fun while doing it.

We also have a goal to sell a lot of Girl Guides cookies. It's a great opportunity to not only raise money for our girl guide troop so we can continue to do the fun activities we look forward to week after week, but it also really taps into our business sense. We each have to come up with the best way to meet our personal cookie sale goals and it really promotes entrepreneurial spirit in young girls. Young businesswomen in the making! The best part about it is that if we do well with our sales, we get to eat one cookie of our choice from the whole variety we sell! You'll always find us with the mint chocolate chip cookies. They are just so delicious! We also have amazing teachers in our Girl Guides troop. They are kind and inspiring and we look forward to attend meetings each week. To mix things up, we go ice-skating class every Wednesday evening. It's something we've thoroughly enjoyed and have been more than happy to stick with, for fun and for fitness.

The only reason for going so detailed on home schooling was to share that the way we defined it does not align with any standard definition. We all have the power to choose what we want to do and too many times we don't connect with that power. So you may be looking at a decision in your life but going off the beaten path may seem full of challenges. Everyone's environment is different and what works for one will not work for another. So choose what works for you, in your unique environment and path, and then work hard to make it happen. This was the best advice we got from our mentors and we designed our experience around it.

The decision to go off the beaten path has brought us so many new opportunities and our vision has grown because of it. It changed the way we react to situations or adapt to conditions that we may not be expecting. That is the only message we have in this book – we all have the power within us and all we have to do is connect with it. You can have fun and make a difference if you really want to.

We believe that if you love something, give it a try. Even if an idea doesn't work out you will be proud that you gave it a try. There is a tendency in all of us to overthink. The opportunity could be gone tomorrow, and we may never have it again because we are worried something better may come along or that something may not go according to our plan! Surround yourself with mentors who believe in you and it will help you take action. If there is one reason for our progress, it is the presence of incredible role models and mentors in our lives who support us every step of the way. You will read about them later in this book.

Now, we will dive into the details of our online art store business (www.twosistersonamission.com). So far you have read about our journey that led us to a point where we really wanted to make a difference. It is in those experiences, those challenges, those failures and those small wins that we found our power and you can too. It is this mindset that we want to share with the larger world.

We wanted to make a difference but we did not know what to do next. All that changed when we went to build a library in a first nations reserve in Canada.

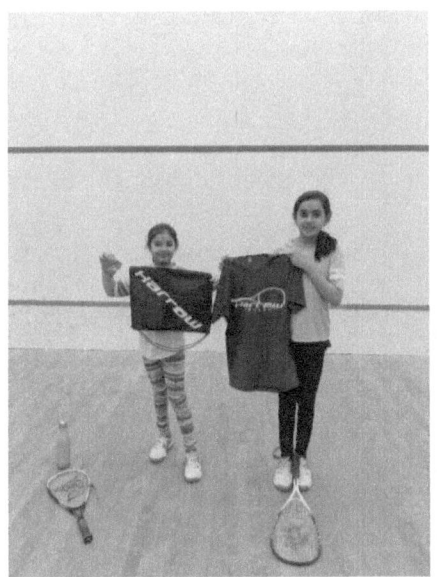 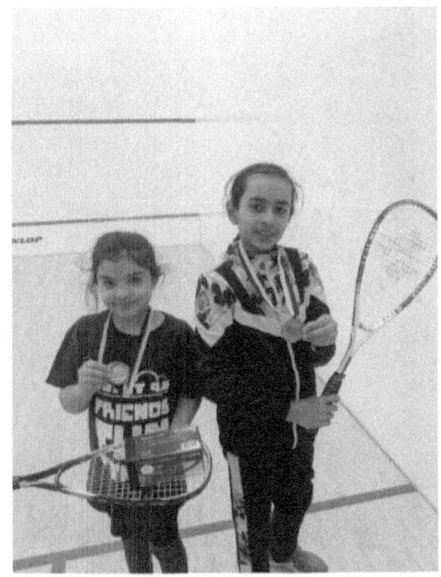

We frequently compete in tournaments across Ontario. It is our dream to play Squash for Canada one day.

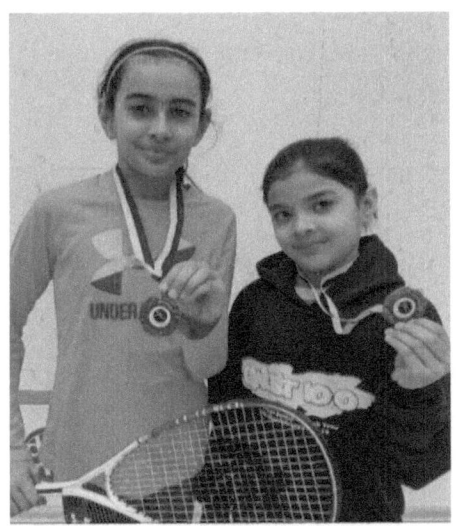 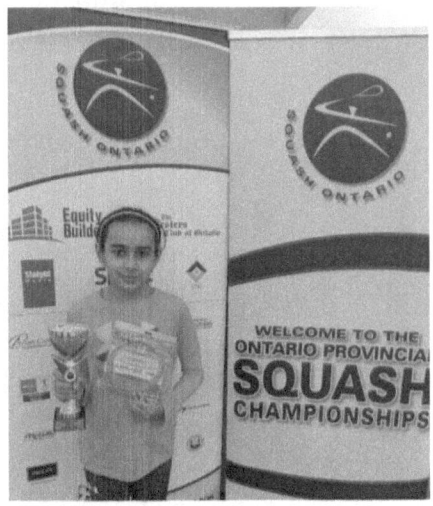

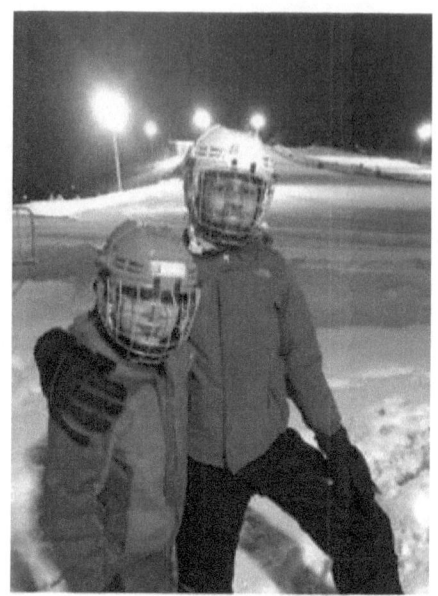
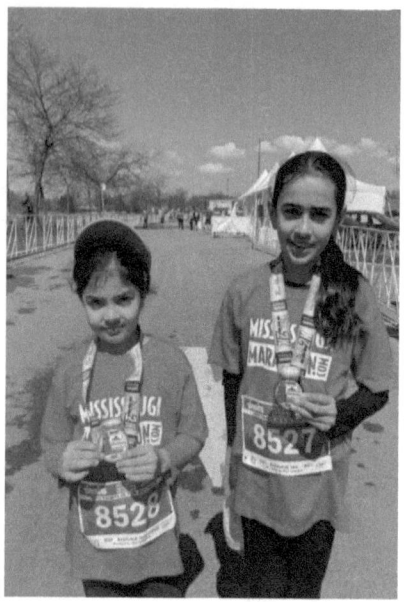

Having fun while making a difference are both possible. After all, anything is possible! (Above left) This is us before going tubing with our Girl Guides group (Right) After our 5km run at the marathon (Below left) Obstacle race filled with mud (Below right) After our timed 5 km run just under 30 minutes

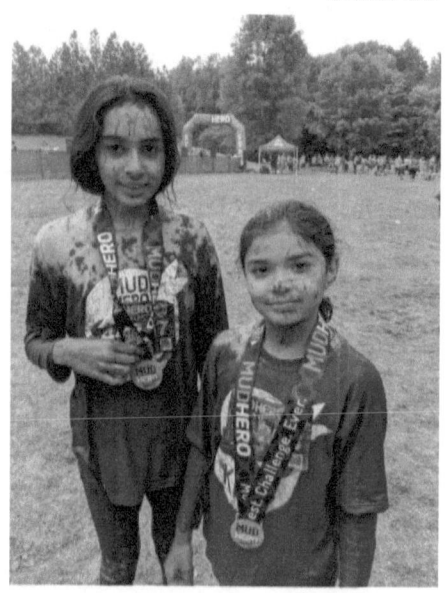
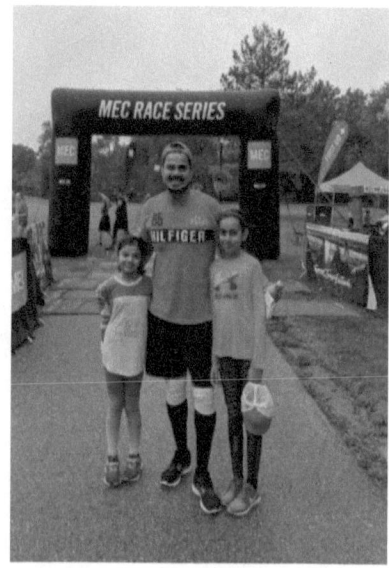

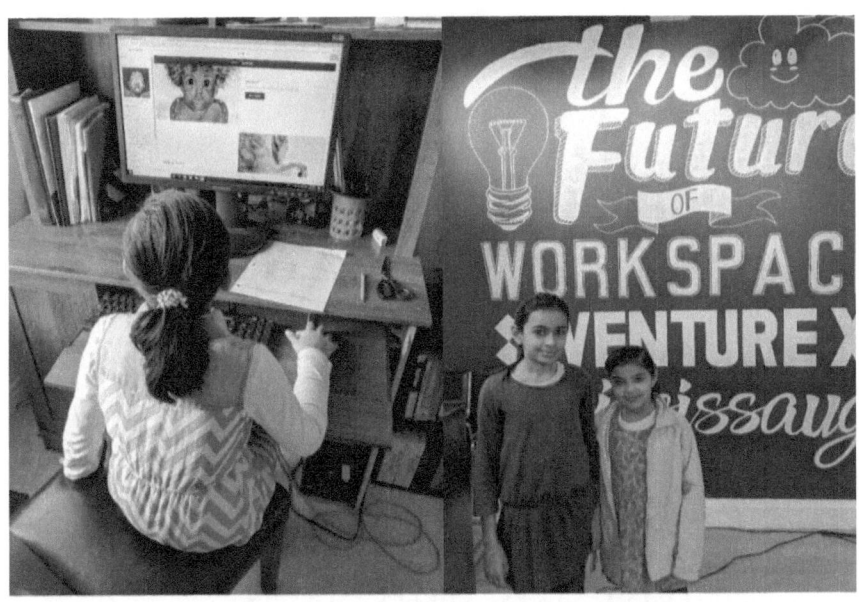

(Above left) Designing our website (Right) Keynote at Venture X Hackathon (Below left) On our way to Google Canada (Below right) Amna working on her studies at a co-working space

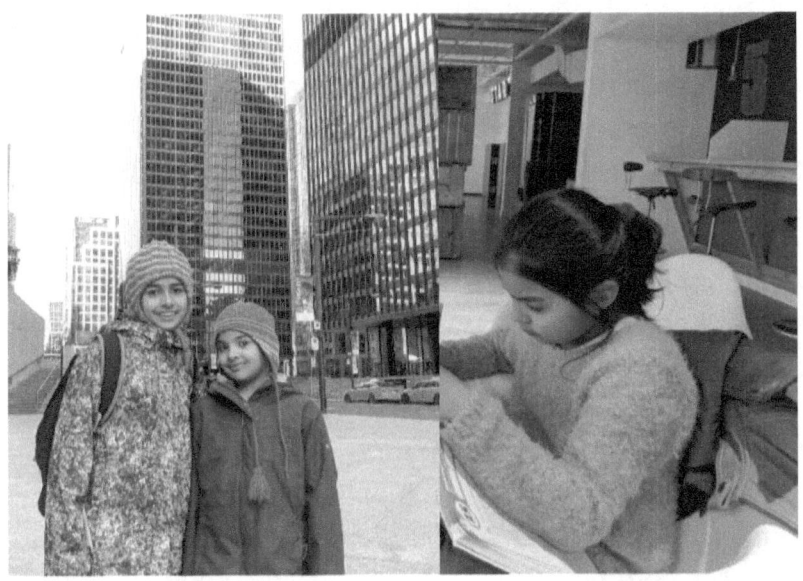

CHAPTER 6: TWO SISTERS ON A MISSION LAUNCH

Building www.twosistersonamission.com has been one of the best experiences of our life. We love everything about our mission, our project and above all our artists. We will speak from our heart as we share the sequence of events that led to us creating Two Sisters on a Mission. When you read this chapter, leave your mind empty and visualize with us the places we describe and the people we meet.

As we shared before, we as a family want to build 100 libraries all around the world. This project is deeply personal to our family. Our dad grew up in poverty and he found bookshops and libraries as a place with no limitations, where dreams could run free and anyone could use the resources to do anything they wanted in life. He became a senior executive who travelled all around the world. He gave that life up and committed to use all that he knew to make a difference. To build 100 libraries with our own hands and local change makers so other youths have a place to dream, to grow and become anyone they choose to be in life. At the time of writing this book, we have built 32 libraries in 9 countries. You can see the videos at www.libraryinaweek.com to bring those moments to life.

Our parents always kept us close to their projects and that is how we went as a family to build a library in first nation communities of Shoal Lake 40 and Grassy Narrows. We didn't know what to expect as we had never been to a reserve and we were greeted with open arms and with so much love. We were welcomed like family and we taught traditional skills like moose calls and how to read the footprints in the forest.

In Grassy Narrows, the Pow Wow ceremony was going on and the drums were loud, it was a magical atmosphere. For those that have never attended a Pow Wow – put it on your list to visit this year. It is an incredible experience that brings together thousands of years of history. During this festival, we met an inspiring individual and his name was Jason Fobister. He had a very positive and calm energy around him. We had a casual conversation with him until something incredible happened. When we told Jason, we were looking for artists, he surprised us and mentioned he was an artist. He told us that his art was spiritual. When he painted, he felt free. He was an artist, painter, dancer, singer and a warrior from the Lynx clan.

Jason showed us his art and what it meant to him. We sat down and listened to everything he said as the first nations songs and Pow Wow drums played out in the background. It was a magical moment. When Jason was explaining his art to us and what the paintings meant to him, it was like he was in his own world and we were so honored that through his descriptions, we were joining him in this world where there was balance and love.

After that conversation we felt excited, motivated and inspired. We knew the world needed to hear his stories as well. In that moment, we thought about launching a business that supports remote artists around the world. That brings their incredible stories, their struggles, their message and their dreams to life. In that moment, we decided to not just let this be an idea but to take action to launch our dream. The world and lives will not change if we wait for others to act, all of us are the change the world needs.

We believe that social entrepreneurship needs to be built on real purpose. We genuinely have to care at a deep level about the problem our business is solving as a social enterprise before we worry about anything else. For us, our artist and their struggle were our inspiration.

We were inspired by Jason's life story and his vision. Jason's painting was visually amazing, but they were so much more than that. We had never been inspired so much in our lives by any artist. We were inspired by him to such extent that we wanted to do something about it. We felt after pens for libraries failed, we had been waiting too long thinking what exactly we should do that will make a difference. Something that can drive positive change. Something that we believe in and it makes an impact on other people. That's when we decided that we shouldn't be waiting anymore. If we don't go after what we want, we will never have it. If we don't step forward, we will never know what we had the potential to do. We knew we needed to take action and to act now. We were inspired by Jason's desire for painting and his love for people. We had learned a valuable lesson from our first failed business that we needed to build a proper business model to achieve our social impact this time around.

We first sat down with our parents and discussed next steps. Our family supported us a lot and inspired us to do the things we were dreaming about. They never doubted our ability to do it, they simply asked what support we needed to get it done. We felt in control and felt that we had the power. We did a lot of discussions and planning. We discussed ideas and concepts on our business model and focused on how we should land this and what would be the immediate next steps. We spent days thinking through this. With so many things going through our mind, we were so grateful to our parents that they supported us in our mission. It inspired us to work hard and be accountable and to do things that matter while having fun and enjoying life in the process.

We wanted to build this business our way. We had seen firsthand through the Experience Your Life Expo the power a good social business has to make a real difference in lives. If it is built on passion, purpose and a good business model then it will make a difference in a way that no other project can.

With a large number of strategies to consider on how to even approach this business, we did a lot of thinking for a few days. There are numerous ways you can approach a problem but making a decision about a specific way is one of the most important things because that is what makes the project real. The life skills we had been learning were now coming to play. We wanted to pick a direction and then start moving fast towards it. We started to really focus on the vision of our business. As a first step, we wanted to create a mission statement that represented our purpose. We did a whole lot of thinking Fatima thought of this phrase, "We want to showcase our artists by bringing their art, their story and their struggle to life". It was a wonderful phrase for our business as it really captured our intentions. But we thought we can come up with more interesting phrases. Amna had come up with another phrase that was deeper. It was "Our mission is to bring the world together." We felt on top of the world as we brainstormed this. It was so exciting. Together, with the grace of God, we felt like a formidable team that can take this task on. To do something that has not been done before. To launch a real business that could one day make it all the way to Dragons' Den and beyond. Our dream was clear but we had a lot of work ahead of us.

Then Amma came up with the idea that what if someone on the other side of the world will feel better after they hear Jason's message and see his spiritual art. How can we connect that person with Jason. We knew that they will never know of each other until we do something about it. We knew we could make a difference in lives by showcasing the incredible work of our artists, their vision and their message to the world. We dreamed of one day illuminating places all over the world with this message just like we had seen kids transform when they had entered bright and colorful libraries. We realized that our mission was best captured if we combined the two statements we had come up with before. We decided to connect the two phrases to create *"Our mission is to bring the world together. We get the artist, their art, their story, and their struggle and bring it to life"*. Our parents loved it. They were very thrilled with our progress.

The next step was to come up with a name for our business. It was a very important step as it captured the identity of our business and would be the foundation of our brand. We wanted to create a brand that reflects our values, our mission and our personalities. We decided on a name that captured all of the above. From the moment we came up with the name "*Two Sisters on a Mission*", we loved it! The first part had us in it and the second part was our vision. This name sparks curiosity and it makes a statement. We loved the business name as this whole process brought us so close as sisters as well. We were very happy about the name of our business. We celebrated for a few hours as this was a big step of our entire process. Now we were officially on a mission to make a difference and we did not want to waste any time. We quickly went forward with the next step of logo design. We wanted to design a logo that truly represented the vision of our business.

We wanted to make a logo that was impactful and communicated our message. So instead of hiring professionals to do it, we decided to pick up a drawing board and brainstorm ideas. After all, we were inspired by our artists and wanted to start this business with creativity. We started brainstorming and thought that our logo must have an earth in it. It represented the concept of bringing the world together. We were not sure how to capture it. So, we tried many different ways to draw it. We believe the only way for you to grow and evolve is to keep trying and keep moving forward. We kept on trying and giving our best shots. We shared the concept with some of our close friends and mentors so that they can share their thoughts. We were really excited to hear from our role model Major Alexia who gave some amazing ideas.

Everybody loved our designs and gave us their thoughts to improve them. In the final design, we decided to hold the earth with our hands because it represents our vision. Now was the time to make our sample design into the final logo.

First, we got a plain white piece of paper. Then we went on the internet for some ideas on how to make earth on paper, so we opened YouTube to view some videos. We kept on drawing till we were happy with the version of earth we wanted. After the 6th time, the earth looked like it should. We were drawing for hours because we were firm on our decision that we would not move until we are done with drawing the earth. We then colored the earth blue and green. Once we finished coloring it we started to draw ourselves.

I (Fatima) drew myself wearing a yellow dress with red dots on it. Then Amna drew her face, hair, and dress. Then both of us drew our hands holding up the earth. Once the design was done we realized that we drew our personalities in it. Fatima is the more focused one who understand number and strategy and Amna is the energetic one all over the place who knows how to connect with people When you look at the logo, see if you can spot us in the logo. We showed the design to our parents, and they appreciated our commitment. Step by step we were making progress. Now all we had to do was convert it digitally. We did not know how to do it but in life everything has a solution. Everything you know right now was once something you did not know how to do before.

We knew we were not the first ones with this problem of converting a hand drawn logo into a digital one. At first we googled a solution, downloaded a software and tried to do it but the results were not that great. In business, we had learned to focus on the important tasks. We went to the website Fiverr and got it converted in less than 24 hours. As a small social business, time is most important thing and we must use it on critical things like sales, strategy and growing our business. Too many times business owners try and do everything themselves and don't end up having anytime to do the really important work. The logo was hand drawn with love and we drew ourselves and how we wanted to express ourselves.

The next step was creating our website. Now that's going to be another step that we must overcome. No matter what, we had to proceed forward because just like the title of this book, we believed anything is possible. Nothing is impossible in the world if you make up your mind. We had learned a valuable lesson from our last business about the importance of finding the fastest way to achieve our desired objective and to not reinvent things that have been invented before. The right tool or strategy can save days or weeks of effort. The business outcomes are not just dependent on how hard you work but rather on how effectively you work. We decided to make our website on Shopify because it will be easier to build and takes less time.

We worked non-stop on creating our website, learning how to configure themes, getting all the right images of our art, creating a YouTube channel where we could keep our videos, selecting the sizes we wanted to promote and so many other details. Slowly seeing our dream come true is a feeling we can't describe.

We requested Jason Fobister to explain each of his paintings in a video. We captured the videos and learned how to edit videos using a simple software. It took a lot of video editing, but it was all worth it. We uploaded the photos, listed the prices, designed the page and picked a theme and created a blog. After a month-long process, we were ready to launch the business. It was not easy but we learned along the way as we were driven by our mission – to make a real difference. It is so important to ground what you do in something that you deeply care about. We cared about our artist. He is family to us. We remembered all the others that we were not able to help as we did not have a good business model before. It inspired us to think through all aspects of our business and drive it to full momentum. We thought carefully about our outreach and marketing strategy and realized that a lot of customers would be professionals. That is why we created a profile on LinkedIn and decide to use that as our primary networking and marketing vehicle. We were proud of our business model as for every print sold, we were giving a royalty to our artist for life. We were also producing the prints through multiple suppliers so after the artist is accepted in the store, they don't have to do anything and get royalties for life. We knew with this model we can make a real difference as the social business grows.

Let us sidetrack for a bit to share an interesting story. Our parents knew that technology provides tremendous opportunities but it can also be a challenge. Especially when young kids get addicted to devices and do not develop essential life skills of communication and how to interact with people socially. Our parents would often show us an environment like bus stations, train stations and coffee shops where everyone would be so involved with their phone that they would not have time to talk to each other. We grew up on a farm just north of Toronto and our activities were making bonfire and chasing each other! We would invite our family friends and have real conversations. We also had to watch out for coyotes and learned how to protect ourselves if needed. We had very little exposure to technology growing up and as we remember that one day in school, we were asked what is internet and we replied, we think it is a phone charger! Fatima was six years and Amna was four years old at the time. It was all part of a strategy to develop our social skills first before introducing technology as a way to drive change in the world and for business purposes. Now we spend quite a bit of time on the computer but it is for focused business tasks.

Our parents always encourage us to focus on the solution and not the problem. We hit many challenges while trying to design the website but we always knew if we kept looking we will find the answer. In this day and age, the answer is usually a google search or a conversation away. It is never the lack of answer or knowledge that prevents action now. We find it is often the doubt that we all as change makers face to take action. Doubt that somehow we are not enough or we will fail. That is why we are writing this book as we want others to take that next step. To give that dream a shot and to understand that the doubt is simply a friend that will stay with us as we go on to do something that has not be done before. It will stay with us, reminding us, that we are outside our comfort zone and that we should be proud of it.

Youths learn by being around environments where they see their power and an opportunity to make a difference. Every interaction played a part in creating Two Sisters on a Mission. We never realized how much we were actually learning in these trips. For example, meeting Alberto in Dominican Republic was an interaction that stayed with us, so did the smiles of the kids in Mexico and the memories of Sofiya in Caribbean.

So coming back to the story of our business launch, once the logo, website, supplier, business card were all done, we decided to open the business with a big bang! It was going to be on 29th September in front of thousands of people at the Expo. Many people fly in for the Expo and we were going to do a pre-launch with those close to us at a very special dinner event the night before. We were so thrilled to welcome executives and change makers from all parts of the world including Singapore, Panama and all over Canada. It was the perfect moment and we were so excited.

During the planning for the launch, we kept thinking about the best way we could bring our artist to life, to bring his story, his message and his journey. Jason is such a wonderful human and we love him, and we wanted to find the best possible way to bring his story and his art to life. Then an idea came to mind – if we want to bring the artist to life for people – how about we invite the artist to be there in person for the big launch? We still remember the feeling when that idea came, and we got on the phone instantly to invite Jason. We were on top of the world when he accepted our invite.

A few days later, Jason arrived in Toronto. We were so excited to see him and picked him up from the airport. This was the first time Jason had been to Toronto and we were honored to show him around. We headed straight to downtown Toronto and had an amazing time walking around and going on top of the CN tower. Neither us nor Jason had gone on top of the CN tower, so it was a very special moment for all of us. We walked on the glass floor (we had never been that high off the ground!). We saw so much of Toronto from the tower and all the building, cars and people looked like a miniature playset. It was a reminder that things can look very different in life and in business and what you see in front of you is not always the only way. Jason was not just our artist, he was a mentor for us and a role model who was inspiring us as we saw him engage with the world with love and respect.

That night, we all sat down in our house and did a small first nations ceremony to bless the business. With that, Jason did the honors of launching the website. It was an emotional moment for all of us and the eyes were full of happy tears in the room. See the video of the business launch on our website as it captures that moment.

After an overnight sleep, one of the best days of our lives started on 28th Sep 2018. Everyone started to fly-in from all over the world including Rob from Singapore who instantly liked what we were trying to do. He was so kind and supportive. He gave us amazing advice and became our customer. It was so exciting to have the support of such an amazing person who believes in our vision. We later found out that Rob was a senior business executive but what meant the most to us was how he was so kind to our idea.

Rob has since then been an amazing mentor, champion, role model and someone we really look up to. He has been with us every step of the way encouraging us to fly. It was a dream come true when one of our role models, Major Alexia, also flew in from Edmonton that day just to be with us. Major Alexia has inspired us deeply and countless other youths all across Canada. We have written her in a chapter later in this book titled the 'Wind beneath our wings'. Youths absorb the energy that is around them and we are so lucky to have amazing role models in our life.

The event was sold out and we were so excited to be in the company of so many amazing people who inspired us. They were so kind and encouraging that we felt we could do anything in this world as we have good people like Rob, Major Alexia, Jason, our parents and so many others around us.

Jason is not just an accomplished painter but also an incredible singer and dancer. He blessed the evening with a first nations honour song using a handmade first nations drum that he brought with him. We also spoke from our heart and it was a very special moment for us. It was amazing to see the people interacting with Jason and we could see our vision of bringing the world together become a reality.

The next day was equally exciting as we got up early and prepared our booth at the Experience Your Life Expo. Nothing had prepared us for the love and support we got, both from volunteers at our booth, the customers and above all our artist. We presented with him again in the breakout room and he moved the audience to tears again with his story, reasons behind each painting and courage. We had all of Jason's nine painting printed and on display. Our volunteers for the booth were amazing!

As soon as the business was launched, we were so excited and focused on making the business grow. It was a priority for us to dedicate our attention towards this for at least 2 hours, every day. We were learning real world skills in a real-world environment. We shared ideas on how to make sales with our mentors and that is when we learned one of the most important words in business - "marketing funnels." With that input and after analyzing all the data, we were able to determine which events, social media, and outreach made the most and least amount of sales.

We learned how to think on the go as no matter how much you plan, there will always be surprises. For example, we got a surprise call to have a booth at an amazing event at very short notice. We had run out of our business cards. We were not expected to visit any event for several weeks but the startup event at the University of Toronto Mississauga was not to be missed.

We sent the reorder to vista-print but we were going to receive them in two days which means that we would not have them in time for the event. We learned our lesson to always have our cards in stock and sometime mistakes are the best way to learn.

Suddenly, an idea popped in our heads - lets at least print the front side of the card at Staples so we would have something to distribute to the people we meet at the event. We transferred the design to our USB and rushed to Staples to get the cards printed in time. We cut them up by hand to prepare 100 cards to take with us to the event the next day. With everything going the way we wanted it to be, we were so excited to be at our first event after our launch. The message that we learned is that there is always a way to move forward towards your objective as long as you are focused on the outcome.

This is how our dream of opening a business came true. It was off the beaten path but that is where, you sometime find the best opportunities to make a real difference. We had no idea it would grow so quickly and will receive so much support. We just focused on our mission and kept on putting one foot after another. Then things started to happen that we did not expect.

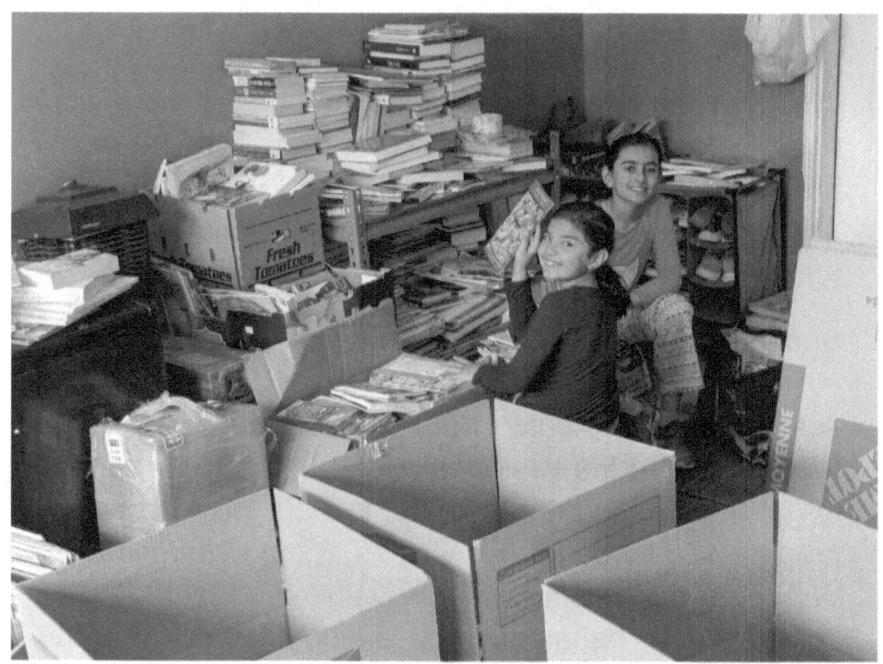

(Above left) Packing hundreds of books for our upcoming build in the first nations reserve (Below) 2500 km from home, we were treated like family and felt at home. The library turned out to be incredible!

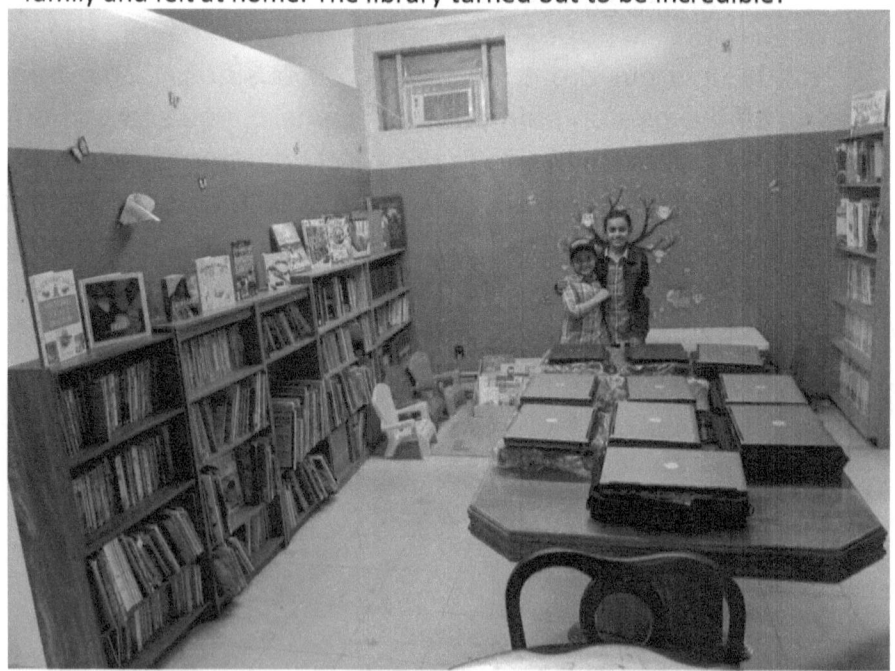

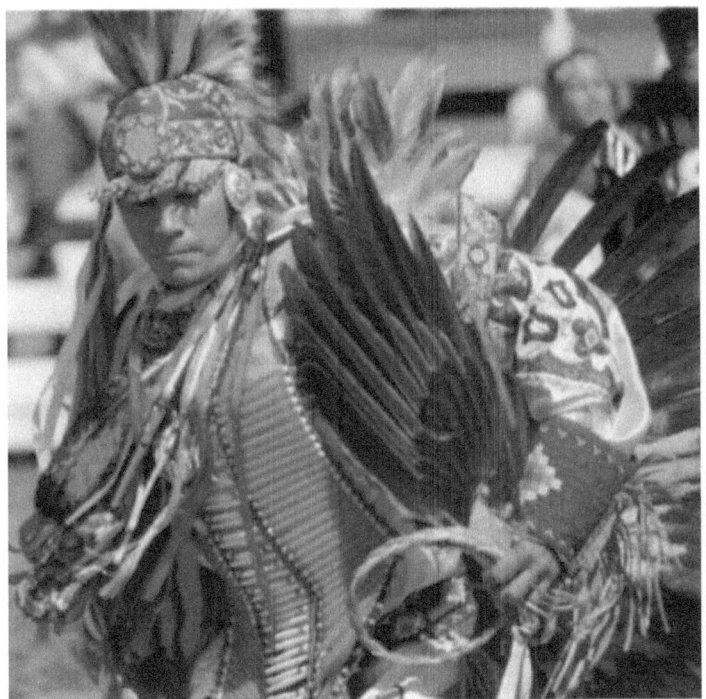

Jason Fobister above. The Pow Wow was going on and the drums were loud, it was a magical atmosphere. His art really moved us. The painting Learning is below as a example. It represents role models who as strong as trees underneath which life can exist.

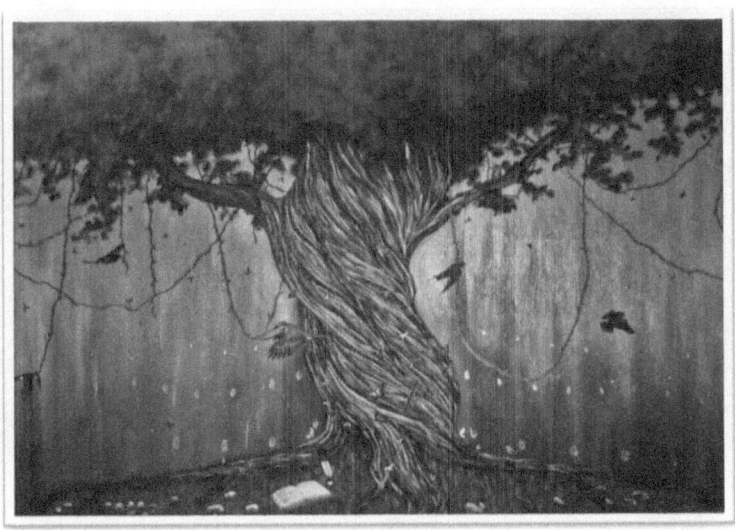

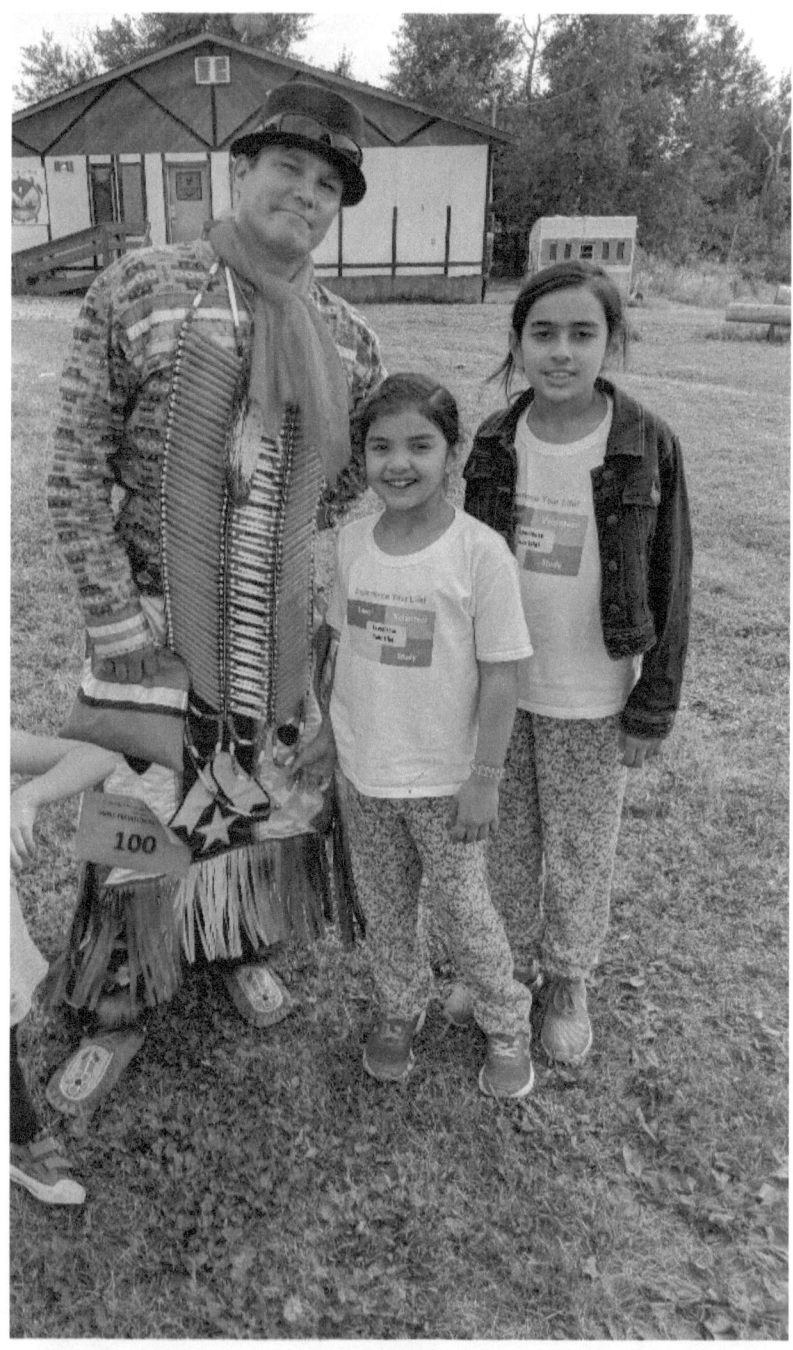

The day we first met Jason. It is a day that changed all of our lives.

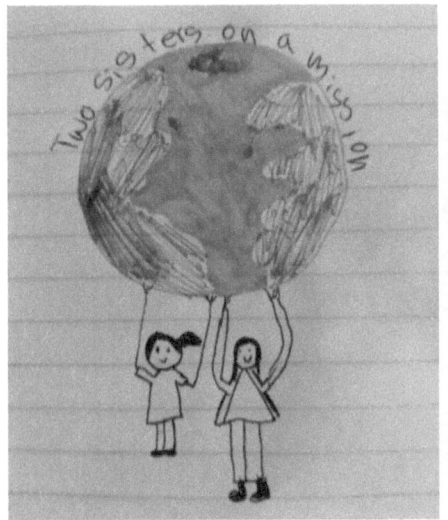
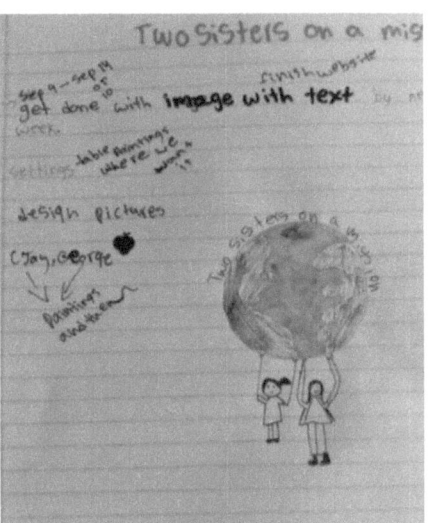

We wanted to make a logo that communicated our message. We worked for hours sketching our different logos. After trying many designs, we thought of one where we were holding the earth

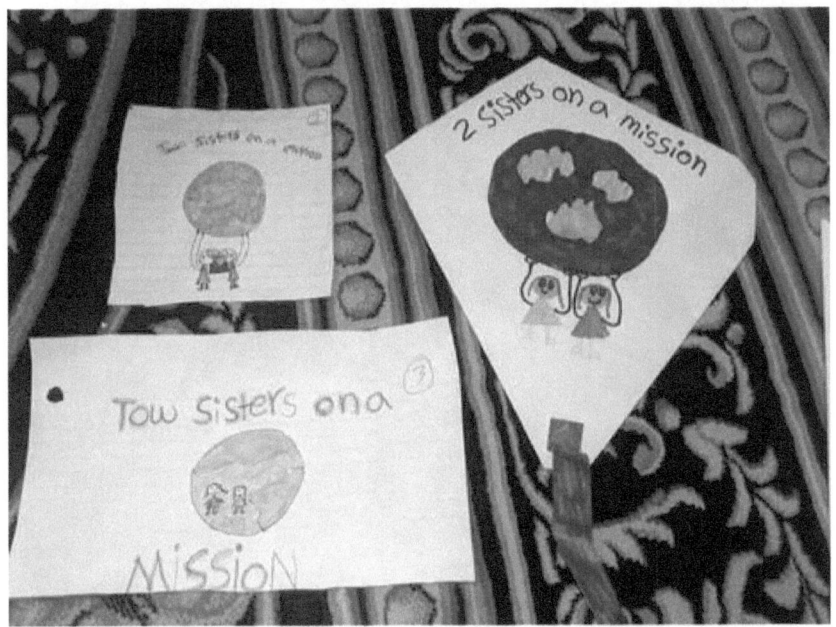

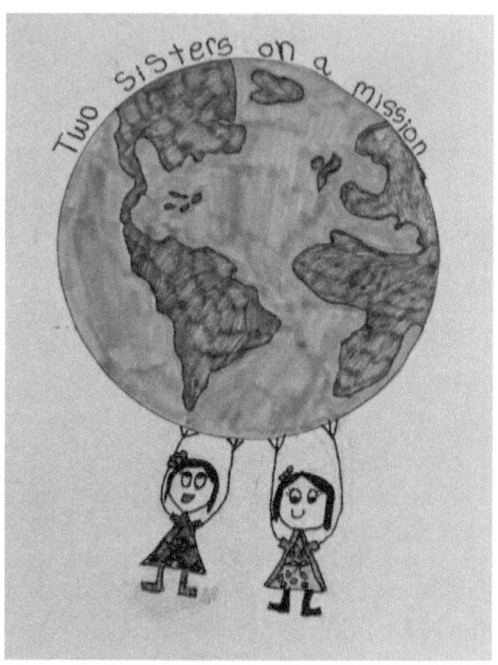

The final hand drawn logo is above! We love it as we worked so hard to make it and that is what makes it so personal and special for us. The digital copy is below

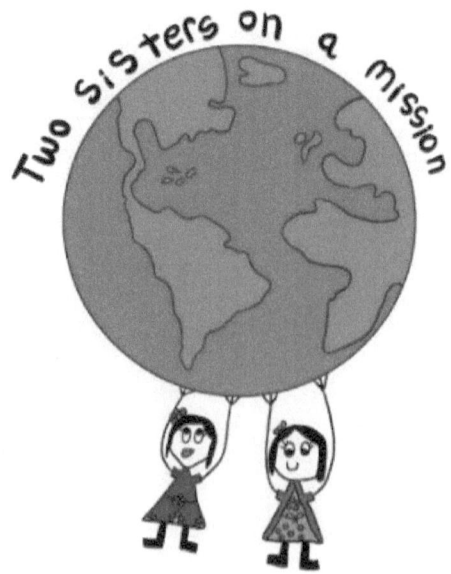

ANYTHING IS POSSIBLE

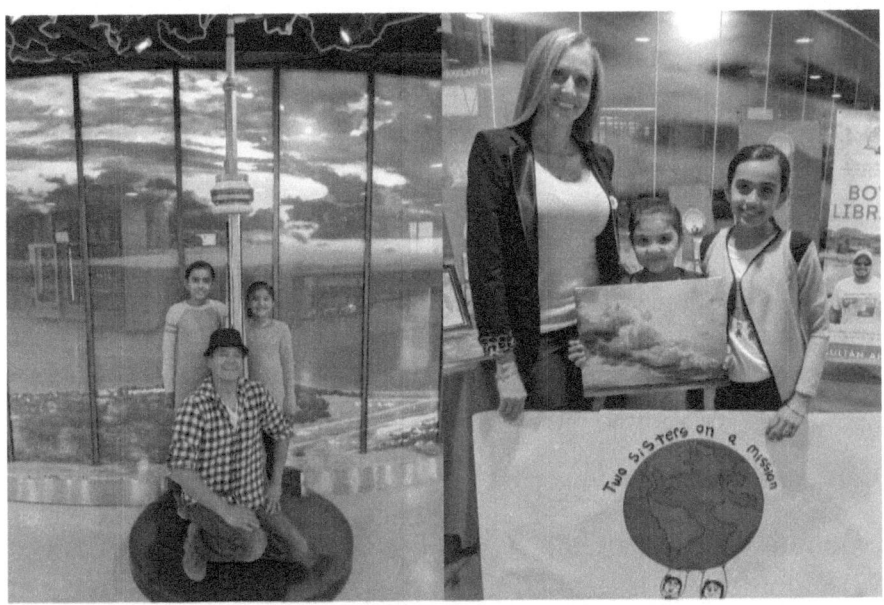

(Above left) Jason and us at the CN Tower (Right) Major Alexia at the pre-launch dinner (Below right) Rob who flew in from Singapore. Surrounded by our role models, we launched our business in front of 200 people!

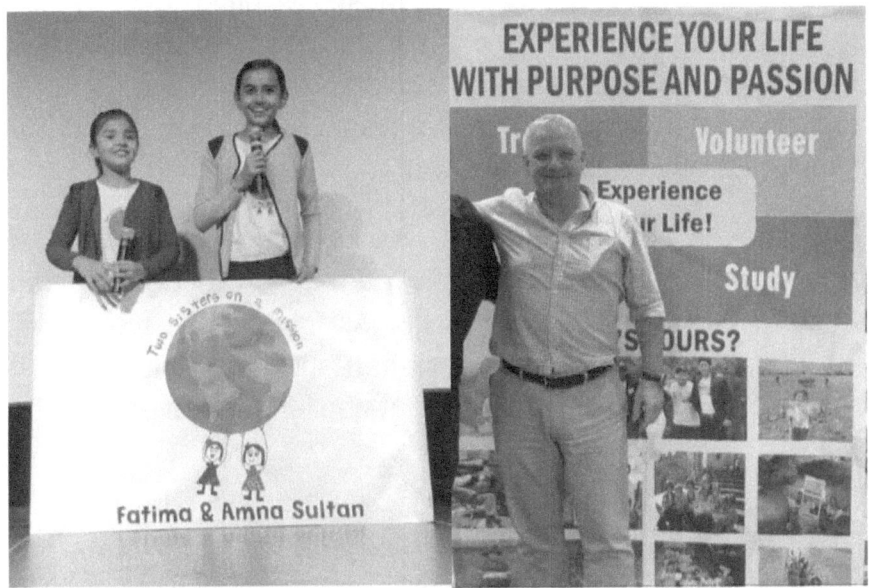

CHAPTER 7: OVERCOMING CHALLENGES

This chapter is about overcoming challenges and the doubt that comes when someone is doing something that has not been done before. We certainly had our challenges and our moments of doubt. We believe that when something is worth doing and you don't think you can, do it anyways! When we try something new, we will face challenges but the reward will be worth it as we will make a difference. While opportunities give us a chance to become excited, the challenges are what really gives you strength. If we gave up after our first failed business, we would have never found out if we could have ever succeeded.

This book is about a mindset. We believe anyone with the mindset of anything is possible can go on to do amazing things. Here are some of the biggest challenges we faced. We describe the challenge and then share the mindset that can help anyone who is facing that challenge to overcome it.

- EXPECT THE CHALLENGES

The first step is to expect that you will encounter the challenges. They should not come as a surprise. When you deal with a challenge, that means you are doing something that you have not done before, you are giving your dreams a chance. Challenges are not something that may happen, they are something that will happen. Being prepared for them and taking them as part of the process was a key skill we learned so that it does not discourage us. If you are not well-prepared in advance, the obstacles that come along the way will dishearten you and distract you from the main goal that you should keep your eyes on. Being prepared does not mean that you will not face any issues along the way, but it means that you have planned how to get rid of those obstacles to reach your final goal.

We knew that we will encounter major challenges in the path of purpose that we had taken. One of the biggest challenges is when we walk into a conference, a business competition or anywhere related to our business, people simply assume we are there to watch. They can't imagine that we have a real business. We find our courage from our role models before us who paved the path for women in business and we fight to establish our credibility and our respect as serious business girls with a big heart. We use real business concepts and explain to those that we are meeting that our business is built on sound foundation. We have a lot to learn still but we have something to offer as well. Once we are able to establish this, we get nothing but incredible support, but it is always a process.

Another very real challenge is that we are not eligible to participate in some of the best competitions around the world because of our age. Our business could be the winner in such competitions and lead to brand awareness and it would be so much easier if we had access to those business competitions. Do you know that 95% of all real business competitions have a minimum age of 18 ?

It is discouraging to feel that we have the power, the revenue, the business insight to win the competition but due to the rules we can't even play. Our role models, including the senior female leaders in law enforcement and technology industries, inspired us by sharing how sometimes they would be the only woman in the room when they started twenty years ago and now they are running big organizations. Challenges are always in the path of those that follow their dreams. Other men and women role models talked about their hardships when they moved cities, schools, universities and had to re-establish themselves. Our message is that we all have the power to redefine the rules.

As of August 2019, we have now spoken in 40 major conferences, competed in major business challenges and got selected for Dragons' Den. We are slowly cutting a path with the support of our mentors. We are thrilled to share that we have been selected as the keynote speakers at one of the biggest economic development conferences in 2020. When you don't have the opportunity to play due to rules, realize that you have the power to create your own rules. We hope to encourage more business competitions to remove the age limit for youths to compete, especially for competitions focused on social entrepreneurships.

It is easy to look at the problem and give up but if the social entrepreneur is driven, they have to find a way. If they are not allowed to be in a competition, then they can make their own. Just because the way things are today, doesn't mean that they have to be that way tomorrow. Society and civilizations have progressed when people challenged the most basic things. So, if you feel that you are not allowed to do something because of a rule that is not fair, then fight to change it. It will take time, but you will enjoy the process.

Powered by this, we are so honored to share that I (Fatima) won one of the biggest speaking competitions in Canada (Youth Slam in Speaker Slam) in the under 18 category as a 10 year old.

- BUILD YOUR COMMUNITY

When you are doing something that hasn't been done before, you will encounter challenges. You will encounter a lot of people who will doubt you, who will simply be so stuck in the way things are that they cannot envision a better future. There is a constant push for change makers to align with what everyone else is doing. The pressure is strong but all is does is make people give up on their dreams. It would be so easy for us to give up all that we are doing and simply do what everyone else does. The challenge is that if you do that, you end up on a back of a very big line. By following everyone else, you give up on your individual power, miss out on off the beaten path opportunities and the fun that comes with doing something exciting and interesting.

The biggest source of strength is surrounding yourself with great role models. Those that inspire you and push you to be the best version of yourself. Those that won't just give advice but whose very presence empowers you. We are so honored to be surrounded by such individuals from Air Force pilots to one of the top female business executives in Canada, from first nations artists to youth leaders, from female police officers to the deans of our biggest colleges. We are surrounded by people that are using their power to raise the spirits of others and empower them. This is our tribe and whenever we need motivation we look to their journey and it inspires us. As we set about doing big things, we started with identifying who is in tribe, who will encourage us and support us to help us achieve our dream. Spend most of your time and energy with the group that empowers you and not discourage you.

- REMEMBER HOW FAR YOU HAVE COME

Our events are growing bigger and so is the audience size. Our business is growing and now we are working with some of the biggest organizations in Canada. Once again, we are two ordinary kids with all of the same nervousness that anyone else would have when they are going to a meeting with senior executives to try and make a deal or the second thoughts a speaker has before going on a stage.

We find a really good way to connect with our power when dealing with a challenge is to reflect back and see how far we have come and how much we have grown. If you can take time to reflect on your development too because looking back at where you were in the past, you feel so joyous to see that you kept moving forward and learned lessons. This gives strength to overcome the next obstacle. For example, just like anyone else we had our doubts taking the stage. The first set of speeches were so hard as we could hardly get our voice out. We felt afraid but we knew we were speaking on behalf of those that were unable to come to that stage. Whose challenges were much bigger than ours and that is what fueled us.

Now, we are being asked to speak at even bigger events and that challenge is still there but seeing how far we have come motivates us. Reflecting on your progress gives a boost to your self- confidence. So, when you feel nervous, remember you are awesome and you have come this far, now is the time to go for it! Believe that anything is possible if you give your full focus, love and attention to the task.

- **MAKE YOUR OWN PATH**

Too many times, we try as humans to be just like everyone else but that is often at the cost of life experiences and dreams that we really want to follow. We had supportive role models who encouraged us to go off the beaten path but also gave us the power to choose the life experiences we wanted. We are really happy doing what we love and making a difference but our message through this book is to encourage youths and adults to find their own power as well.

We have a very active social schedule filled with fun with our own age group in after school programs and we are fully engaged in immersive learning experiences such as opening electronics up to see what is inside. We love selling cookies for Girl Guides as much as we love engaging in real business deals and solving real business problems. We love speaking as much as we love listening and learning. We love to work from universities and college campuses and at the same time we love to do all the things that other kids do in terms of summer fun. We just came back from a six-week break in which we did nothing but have fun. Now we are working non-stop on our goals and our book. This doesn't fit into a box or a defined role. Our message is that we all have the power to choose how we spend our time.

So sit down today and ask yourself what things in your life are things you are doing that you absolutely love. Then decide to do those things more. Remember you have the power to make that choice.

Our dad gave up his job as a senior technology executive to create a life which allows him to spend a lot of time with us and still find the time to follow his dream of building libraries and events that change lives. Our mom loves to volunteer in different organizations and also spends a lot of time with us. We learned from them that life is a gift and we all have the power to choose experiences on a daily, weekly, monthly and yearly basis that fill us with joy and purpose. Don't be afraid to do what is different if you enjoy it and remember you can create your schedule. It's worth it!

- BELIEVE IN YOURSELF

As we touched in the topic above, one of the biggest challenges we faced is to be taken seriously in business competitions in the beginning. When we pitch, everything changes. Like many before us, we are proud of representing a change. Our message is that you are never too old or too young to follow your dreams. If you believe in it, go for it. It is that simple.

We want to share this mindset with youths around the world through this book. To encourage their creativity and help them trust themselves and never to give up on their dreams. The best advice to all youths around the globe is that they should not be afraid to follow a career they love. You can be whatever and whoever you want to be, a teacher, a photographer, a footballer, a businesswoman, and most importantly a humble human being who knows what to do with their power. Whatever inspires you, you should do it. There are no boundaries that can confine an empowered young person.

We continue to face challenges to grow our business, find new clients, find new artists but we have fun doing it as we believe in our impact. When you connect with your purpose and create your project, you will feel the same way. It's not about us, it's the mindset that unleashes the power.

- **HAVE FUN**

We want to change the world and have a LOT of fun doing it. Changing the world can be fun and exciting. We love what we do and the bigger message is that when you start a project, think through how this would impact your life, how will you end up spending your time and if you are going to enjoy the process.

Most afternoons we head to squash or girl guides depending on the day. In addition, we try and learn a new skill every week such as editing videos in Filmora, playing around with a new theme on Shopify or a brand-new shot in Squash and learning how to ice-skate. When you learn, you use your mind and you grow as a person.

There are many things in business or in life that you have to do so that you can enjoy the fun parts even more. For us, driving long distances to events or sometimes waking up early to go to a big conference can be a bit hard, but when we are on the stage, or at the event, the feeling of excitement takes over. Our message is to really think through how you can create a schedule in which you are able to have impact, have the life experiences you like and still have a lot of fun doing it. We are building our business such that we can work from anywhere and sometimes that is exactly what we do. We go to different universities and colleges and work from there. As part of immersive learning, we do fun things like talking to people we don't know and getting to know them. Navigating through a big university campus is like a treasure hunt. The best way to overcome the challenges that come with a social business is to have a lot of fun doing it!

- ## CHOOSE YOUR MENTORS CAREFULLY

One of the biggest challenges when you go after something big is that every person is going to have an opinion on how you should do it. We get advice all the time from random strangers at events to extended friends. It can get tiring. Many people give advice without actually having been through the experience themselves or through our website. You have to pick your role models and when you engage with someone about your business or idea, be very careful. There is nothing more draining then doubt being planted next to a good idea before it has even grown. There is a difference between creating doubt and having good advice that challenges your idea and helps it grow. The difference is that folks in the second category will be with you to help you drive the outcomes, they will respect your decision and they will help you find your power rather than give you solutions.

We learned the importance of selecting our mentors carefully early in our business and lives. We are lucky to be surrounded by great people. These individuals don't tell us what to do but guide us through bouncing ideas and simply giving us the space to grow and make our decision. Being with us when we fall down and cheering us on when we succeed. The point of this is to be careful who you keep in that circle and to understand that when you are doing something that has not been done before, most will doubt you and listening too much to that advice may lead you to doubt yourself. Believe in yourself and surround yourself with those who believe in you.

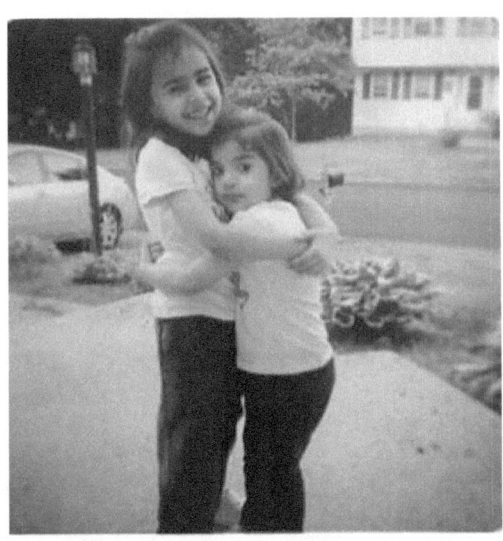

(Above) The Two Sisters can never be separated. We are not just sisters, we are also best friends (Below left) At our very first Experience Your Life Expo as project managers. We were 6 and 4. (Below right) Three years later we competed at Vaughan Social Innovation Challenge to come in the top 10 companies

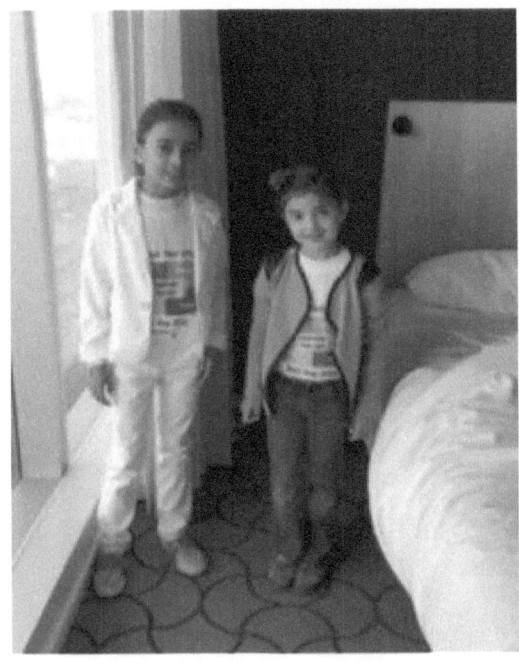

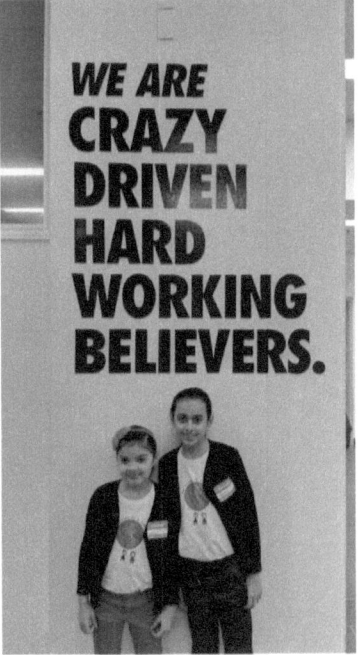

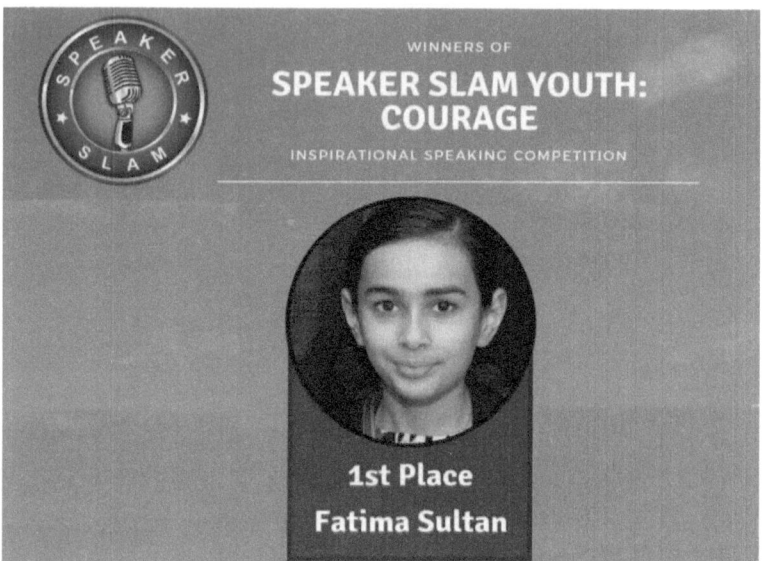

(Above) It was such an honor to win first place at one of the biggest speaking competitions in Canada in the under 18 category. My speech was "You Are Enough" and I spoke from my heart and it resonated with the audience and judges. (Below) We participated in an angel investor summit and heard businesses pitch for money. It was really interesting

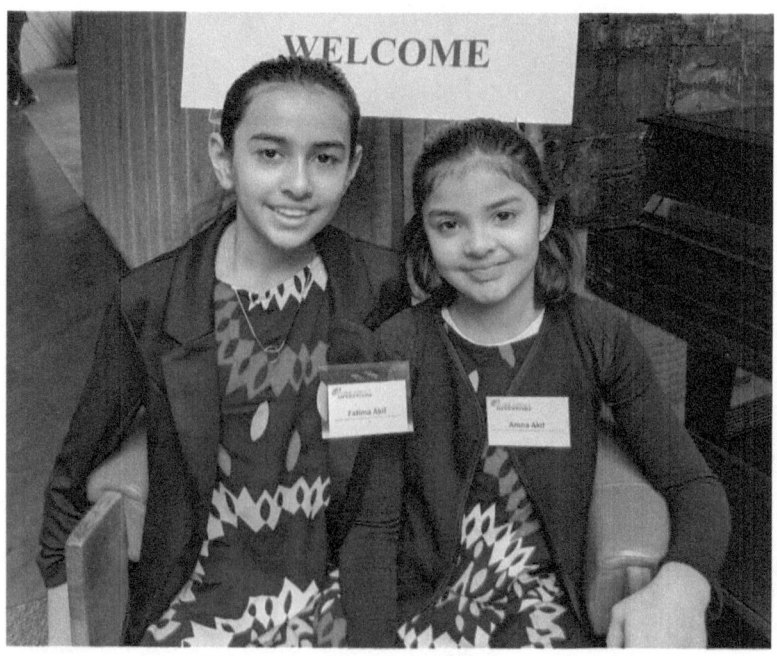

CHAPTER 8: FACING THE DRAGONS

"Hello – I am from the production team at Dragons' Den, may we speak with Fatima & Amna Sultan?". We got on the phone right away not sure what to expect.

"Is this Two Sisters on a Mission?" she said. "Yes, this is us, how are you?" We replied simply not sure what words to use to keep our excitement in check. "I am doing great and you are about to as well, you have been selected in the very few companies out of the thousands to come and pitch in front of the Dragons. I am calling to book your filming date!". I don't think we have ever screamed that loudly with excitement on the phone. Ever!

Let's take a step back to what led to that phone conversation. After our business launch, we started getting a lot of request from events and organizations to speak about our story. We were really nervous at the beginning, but we knew that this was not about us, but rather a message that could empower many people to go after their own dreams. We found our power by thinking about our artists and we were so grateful to so many organizations who welcomed us with open arms. We shared stages with professional speakers, CEO's of major organizations and change makers who we looked up to and every single time we learned something amazing from both our fellow speakers and the audience. It was not just about us sharing our journey but about us absorbing that incredible positive energy and we were learning so much in the process.

We are honored to share that at the time of publishing this book in September 2019, we have done keynote speeches around the world at major conferences including Microsoft DigiGirlz. You can see the full list on our website, but this book is not about that. It is about helping every reader to tap into their own power to get their own chain reaction started.

So, after the launch of our business, things were going great but one of the biggest challenges a social entrepreneur faces is finding out about the biggest opportunities. Many opportunities simply pass by without us ever knowing about them. That is where surrounding yourself with good people really helps. We were just going about our business without having Dragons' Den on the radar at all – it was just too big a dream to even imagine. It was one of our favorite shows for years.

We were watching an episode of Dragons' Den online and then saw the notification that the deadline to apply for stage 1 of the auditions was only a few days away. We were feeling completely unprepared, did not have a clue how to compete at that level, felt completely intimidated by the size of the platform and the fact that we were attempting something that has not been done before. We had all the reasons to simply keep moving on and not give this a try. Then we asked ourselves, what is the worst that can happen? We don't get invited? Well, that will happen anyways if we walk away so why don't we give this a good shot? After all, anything is possible.

So with support from our parents we got to work and prepared a pitch. The stage 1 of the audition happened all around Canada and was open to everyone. Thousands of companies pitch at this stage and you have a few minutes to connect with the producers. We always believe that you don't control the outcome but you have control over giving this your best shot. So, we took our all our props, our best paintings, prepared a pitch and went bright and early to the CBC building on the very first day the auditions opened. We were number 7 in the entire country to be standing in that line. If you are going to give something a shot, why come late?

The pitch went well but we had no idea if we will make it from the thousands to a select few that get the chance to pitch on the Den. A few weeks passed by and we gave up on the idea that we made it to round 2. We did not feel sad as we had given it our best shot. That is when this phone call came, and we were on top of the moon. At the time of this book being published, the episode has not gone on TV so we can't disclose what happened. We look forward to setup a watch party when it does take place so we can all see it together!

Our journey is continuing, and we are grateful to the opportunity to make a difference through our social business. We have been confirmed as keynote speakers for one of the biggest economic development conferences in Canada. This conference will have representation from economic development departments from many cities. We will share our story and our deep belief that any youth has tremendous potential to make a difference if given a chance. We must all do more to give youth a chance to find off the beaten path opportunities so they can make a real difference.

We learned so much from our mentors and continue to learn from them. Several are featured in the next chapter. In this chapter, we want to summarize a few points that inspired us to go after our dreams. These are lessons that we learned from our role models and mentors. Sometimes these lessons came in the form of advice, sometimes simply by observing them go after their own dream, sometimes it was in their acts of courage in doing something that had not been done before or sometimes it was just someone with nothing in terms of financial resources having a big smile on their face. We saw and we learned, and it is a perspective that can really help people around the world. So how does a youth or anyone looking to take action go from having an idea to having an impact? Here are five points we learned that can help:

1. TAKE ACTION

   Taking action today, this week, this month is the most important part to get started. The change may be big or small, but it will make a difference. It is the little things that make a big difference. When we started doing Pens for Libraries business it was a small step that failed but we learned so much from it. It took us down the path we are on right now. Taking action, big or small, is the most important part. Having a big dream is awesome but having a bigger list of actions to make that dream a reality is even more important. It is actions that bring real happiness in life and taking action takes courage.

   Courage is not just doing things that look scary. Courage is not just running faster on a well-travelled path. Courage is finding the power to move forward when you are afraid. Courage is not just about big moments but about the little battles you win every day. Courage is about dreaming of what the world can be without being limited by the challenges it has today. Courage is speaking up, fighting for what you believe in, and being the voice for those that cannot speak right now.

   The word courage inspires us. We found ourselves in many situations where were not sure about our abilities and felt doubt, like going in front of the biggest audience we have ever faced, facing the dragons with their questions getting increasingly detailed on business concepts and competing against serial entrepreneurs three times our age in business competitions. In those moments we remind ourselves to be courageous. To put fear aside and focus on our purpose, our reason, our drive to make a difference. We do what we do because we care about those it impacts. That's it and that is what matters. When we focus on that, fear goes to one side and we are only focused on giving our best shot regardless of the outcome.

We have a painting called Courage in our art store which captures this as well as another one called "We Are Warriors" with images of warriors in the clouds reminding us all that we have within us a spirit that is strong.

2. THE TIME IS NOW

We always get asked the question of what inspired us to start our social business at the age of 9 and 7. There are always so many reasons and excuses to not take action that we all surround ourselves with. Too young, too old, too inexperienced, too experienced, not enough degrees, too many degrees, too far, too hard, too complex and the list goes on. We believe the biggest risk is keep on doubting yourself and keep believing those that say you can't do it. Our message is simple – the time is NOW! Whatever it is that you love doing, do it. You can do it in a way that you have a lot of fun and create a new path filled with happiness and impact. That is our goal and we are loving this journey.

Whenever we doubt ourselves, we remember the kids just like us that we met around the world who need our help. We believe that you shouldn't wait to change the world or wait for someone else to act. People are in need and we all have the power to do something. It is an amazing time to be a youth. The opportunities are endless but what holds us back as youths is believing that we are not smart or experienced enough to have an impact. Many kids, teenagers and adults are breaking this image by going after big dreams and achieving them. If you believe in something, go for it. Today, after putting this book down is the perfect time to take the first step.

3. WE ALL HAVE THE POWER

As humans, we end up creating four walls around us with doubt and those walls are not real. The power is within our reach. There is a chant that we say at the opening of every library, which is a promise you make to yourself. "I am strong, I am smart, I have the power to change the world." We did this chant with youths all around the world from Mexico to First Nation reserves in Canada. Over 500,000 people around the world have chanted this with us. It is something we believe in as a family.

If you want to be the best soccer player, it isn't how much equipment you have, it is the will power in your head. We watch a lot of inspirational movies about how people overcome their challenges such as the girl who lost an arm in a shark attack and continued to be a surfing legend. Pele is another good example as he grew up in poverty. His will power was what made him a soccer legend. These role models are like lighthouses. As they light up, they help so many without even knowing about it.

As a family, we believe that every person should have a place to dream and the tools to make those dreams a reality. We were honored to go to the Museum of Human Rights in Winnipeg and we met the CEO who showed us around. We saw the exhibit of Nelson Mandela and how he won with love and courage. It inspired us and we wrote a letter to him as part of the exhibit. It thanked him for inspiring us to go after our dreams too.

We are so honored to follow in the footsteps of so many giants before us who paved their own paths. The brave women in the past knew they deserved the right to vote, and they made sure they raised their voices for that recognition. Major Alexia is such an inspiring woman who continues to tell us to aim for the sky and higher. Those that made history stood up for what they believed in. We all have the power to do that.

4. WE CAN ALL FLY

Our parents worked really hard to help us see the doubt that we would surround ourselves with sometimes. They reminded us that the doubt is what pulls will pull us to the ground and not let us fly. Every person who has achieved success in this world had to break their chains and go after their dreams. Helen Keller is a perfect example for this. Even though Helen was deaf and blind, she continued her journey and left a legacy.

Youths have the power to change the world. Too many times the youth are discouraged and not taken seriously about pursuing their dreams. We all start believing these limitations that are not real. All we need to do is remind ourselves of youths that changed the world. For example, another one of our role models is Terry Fox and his story is so inspiring. He was a young person who found the courage in hardship to follow his dream. Even though he battled with cancer he decided to run across Canada. He left a legacy that continues well after him. Every year people all across Canada run to raise money for cancer research. It all started through Terry. He was a young person with a vision and a dream. The Keilburger brothers started their work when they were only in their early teens and now they have impacted so many lives across the world.

Our role models have one thing in common – they do things that matter. They find the courage to do things differently. They help the human civilization move forward. Doing things that matter could be example like the well-known ones like Terry Fox, Helen Keller and Nelson Mandela's but it can also be everyday actions that matter to someone. We are surrounded by change makers who not only do big things but also small ones. They do it not for the recognition but rather the satisfaction of knowing that their actions matter. You will read about them in the next chapter but what you may not know is that Major Alexia is spending her own time and effort to load an entire helicopter with books to fly to a remote first nations reserve. Sharon went out of her way to introduce us to WE foundation. Karen volunteers at Microsoft DigiGirlz to inspire young girls to follow a career in technology, Rob sponsored a library for children he had never met. We see this most clearly in our own parents as they work so hard to physically build each library with their own hands and local volunteers.

Whether doing something that matters leads to becoming an organization like Terry Fox foundation or it stays as a one-time action, it matters! All legends have one thing in common, they do things that matter. We watched a movie once, based on a true story, of girls not being allowed to compete professionally in the sport of wrestling. Their parents believed they could break the barriers that existed in the society and wanted to give their daughter the same opportunities as everyone else. The girls despite all opposition from society went on to become international athletes winning many gold medals in international wrestling competitions.

5. **REASONS MATTER**

We all know leaders who have made a difference in their unique ways. They all had one thing in common. They genuinely believed in their message and their actions. That is why they were able to inspire people around them. Our mentors taught us that we all have the ability to be leaders in this world. A good leader is humble but not timid, and willing to speak up for what he/she believes in. A good leader is strong but knows that strength is only to help others. A good leader is not afraid to shine their light but their only purpose is to light up others.

Leadership is not about having a group of followers. It is not about being popular or being the strongest. It is about being strong enough to lift others. It is not about just being the fastest runner beating everyone else on the beaten path but rather being the one who is willing to cut a path, and face the challenges of being the first one, so that others have a better chance at following their dreams. Leadership is not about wanting followers but believing so strongly in your actions that it inspires thousands and millions to take action too. We believe youths are limitless and we hope through this story, more will give their dreams a shot.

When we all do something in life for the right reasons, it leads to joy. There is a painting in our art store called "Joy." It captures the incredible laughter of some of the children from Africa. Even though many people in Africa are facing a variety of hardships, the painting shows how happy the kids are in the moment. In our travels, we saw how happy the children were with basic toys or inventing games with stones and sticks. The laughter was real and so was their joy. By spending time with us, they taught us to be grateful and real.

Now we are thrilled to share the best chapter of the book. This is the one in which we get to recognize some of the mentors who have shaped our journey and inspired us to go after our dreams. They represent the hundreds that are now part of our tribe and by reading this book, you are joining it too.

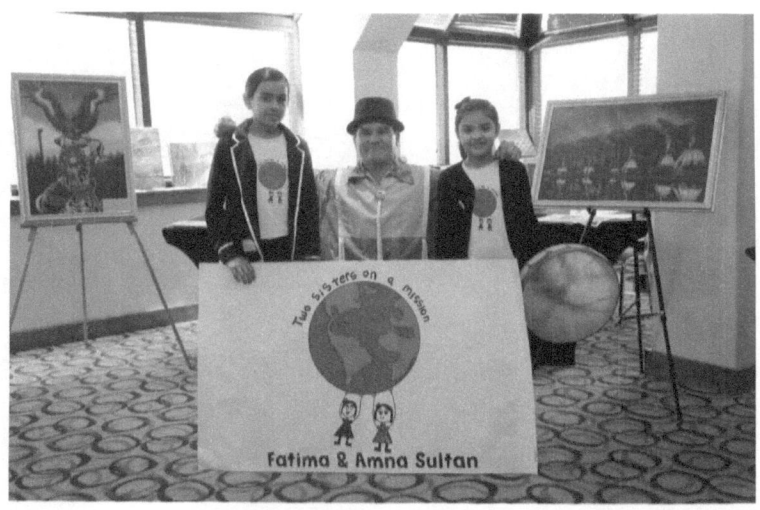

(Above) Jason is not just our artist, he is like family to us. He is one of the most sincere and genuine people we know. He lives 2500 km away but flew in for the launch of the business and will be there at the launch of this book. (Below) The silence before a big event. We use that time to remind ourselves why we are taking the stage. It is about making a difference. In that moment, we feel the presence and support of our artist, our mentors and the kids we met in our journey.

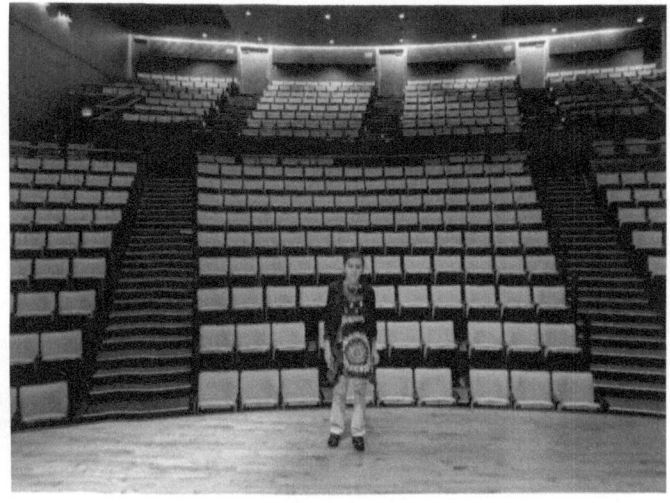

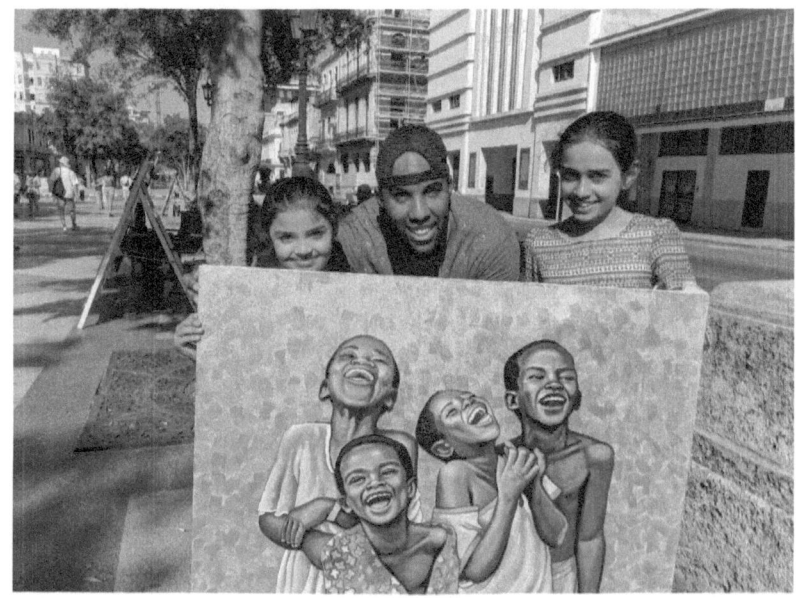

Our artists inspire us. (Above) with Yasmani and the painting 'Joy'. (Below) Yasmani is going through a sketch and fueling our creativity in the process.

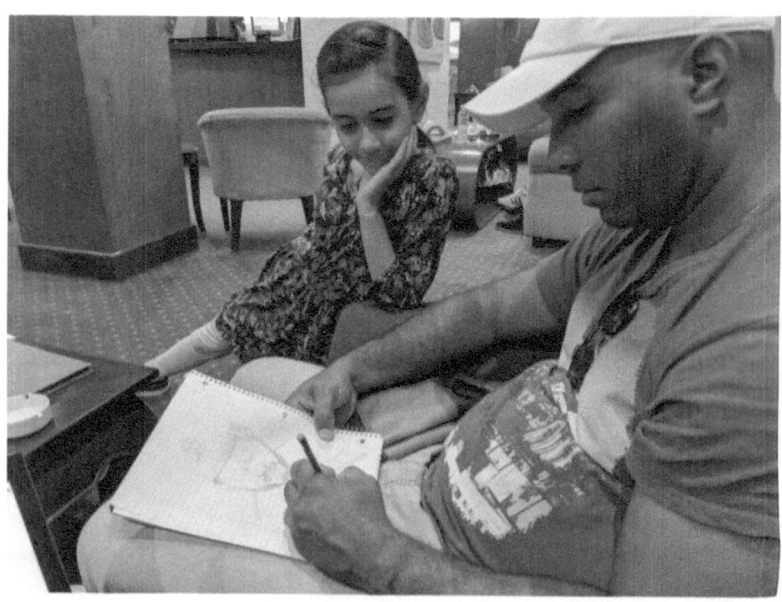

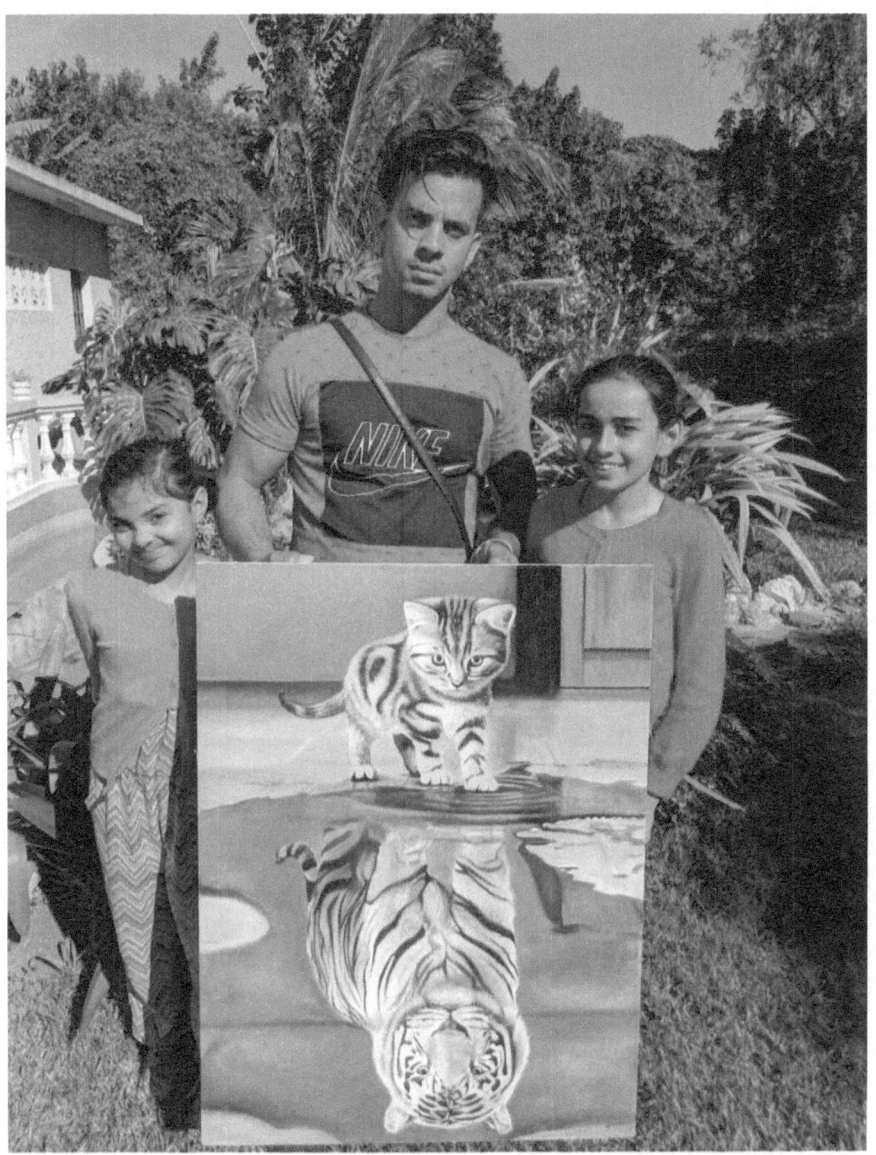

Daviel is an amazing artist but above all an amazing person. He paints from his heart and together with his partner Liliana and their family they gave us so much love. This is the painting 'Courage'

CHAPTER 9: THE WIND BENEATH OUR WINGS

This chapter is our favorite as we get to recognize the amazing, selfless and inspirational role models and mentors who have helped us get this far in life. People who have inspired us to go after our dreams. Our parents believed in surrounding us with role models whose very presence would inspire us. The don't just give advice, they also follow their own dreams thus inspiring youths to follow theirs. For all those that work as mentors with people of any age, that is the only thing we will share from a young person's perspective. We learn so much by being around people who are following their dreams and encouraging others to follow theirs. The best advice is given through the actions of the role model. Surround yourself with people who are strong enough to raise others on their shoulders.

There are a lot of people who have helped us reach this far, literally hundreds and we are grateful to each and every one of them. They are many people who take action with us like event organizers who invite us to present, senior executives who gave us their valuable time for a 'cup of milk' (our version of a business coffee meeting!), youth leaders who paved a path for girls and boys like us to give our dreams a shot, and above all to so many strangers who showed us kindness and compassion during our travels. We are grateful to each and every person who has supported us and took action with us. Their constant support motivates us to strive further in life. Each act of support is acknowledged and appreciated. It might be a direct support backing two sisters on a mission in terms of being a customer, volunteering with us, or it may be a small acts of kindness by sending us supportive notes filled with positive energy.

These individuals have been part of our life for 5 years through this whole journey! We want to take time and highlight a few of these mentors present in our life. From doing big things like flying across the world to come to our business launch to doing little things like sending us a message before a big speech, these individuals are the wind beneath our wings that inspire us and we constantly feel their presence.

Our Parents

Our parents are our biggest role models. They are the coolest people we know, and they created an environment around us that helps us grow. They didn't just tell us what to do in life but showed us through their own actions, sacrifices and dreams.

Knowing that your parents are working so hard for your success inspires you to be the best version of yourself and to make them proud. When you can see how hard someone is working to give you a chance in life, the chance they never had, it inspires you to go after your dreams and to support them in achieving theirs.

Our dad, Sultan Akif, is an award-winning social entrepreneur, author and speaker. Prior to doing what he does now, he was a corporate executive for 17 years who has traveled to over 75 countries. He learned a lot from his career, but his passion remained helping people around the world who needed his help. He left his comfortable career and dedicated his life to make a real difference in lives of people.

He is now the CEO of Experience Your Life Expo, which is the largest youth employment, empowerment and entrepreneurship event in Canada. The Expo was in the national finalist list of the Canada Volunteer Awards which is one of the highest honors Government of Canada gives to any business that is having social impact. He is also the founder of Library in a Week and has built 32 libraries in 9 countries with his own hands and local volunteers. As you read in previous chapter, being part of different libraries builds inspired us tremendously. It is an amazing feeling to see how we all have the power to make a difference if only we find the courage to connect with our deeper purpose. He builds these libraries because he was a boy who grew up in extreme poverty, surviving on less than 50 dollars a month for years and access to books changed his life. You can see the projects at www.experienceyourlife.ca , www.libraryinaweek.com and www.sultanakif.com.

Our mom is an inspiration. We love her very much and she works so hard to give us the best chances in life. With her presence in our lives, we truly feel loved and cared for. Her dream is to make a real difference in this world and for us to have the best opportunities in life. We are lucky to be part of someone's dream and you feel that love around you unconditionally. Our mom creates an environment around us that empowers us with love and inspires us to be the best version of ourselves. We may be tired and exhausted after a long day of speeches, events and studies, but we know that our mom will be there for us with love and care. Our mom loves to celebrate the small moments in life, the ones in which you smile, laugh and make fun of each other. It grounds us to experience the small moments while having the dream to change the world. In combination, our parents provide us with the environment that allows us to go after our dreams.

Seeing our parents work hard on social projects, not cutting corners, keeping purpose at the center of the project and taking care of people inspired us to do the same. They have taught us many things, but the biggest lesson has been to always believe in ourselves. They believe in us unconditionally and that inspires us. They are our cheerleaders, our champions, driving us to all the events and always in the crowd cheering us on. In our keynote speeches, you will often hear them scream with joy as the applause or standing ovation erupts. They always remind us to stay sincere to our mission – nothing else matters. To never let fame or fortune get in the way of impact. To understand that a sound business model is the most effective way to drive impact but ultimately, impact is what we need to focus on. Our dad's speeches have been heard by millions of people all around the world but we never saw him lose his focus in the fame. He loves to put on his shirt filled with paint and work with his own hands to build the libraries.

In our parents, we found the perfect role models that inspires us to stay grounded, enjoy the moments while dreaming to change the world. They inspire us to reach for the sky, to make a difference but yet enjoy every day.

Major Alexia Hannam – The woman who taught us to fly

Major Alexia is the Commanding Officer of the 417 Squadron of the Royal Canadian Air Force. Here is the video from the Air Force sharing the story of this incredible leader https://www.youtube.com/watch?v=6w2lWrjtgyM

She was born and raised in Winnipeg, MB and joined the Royal Military College of Canada immediately after finishing high school. She graduated in 2006 with a Bachelor of Arts Degree in Psychology and a Minor in History. After completing pilot training on the Slings by Firefly, the Harvard II and the Jet Ranger, she spent seven years at 408 Tactical Helicopter Squadron in Edmonton flying Griffon Helicopters.

Major Hannam has been in the RCAF for the last 18 years and she has completed several rescue missions and was deployed during the Fort McMurray and BC wildfires as the Detachment Commander responsible for all Griffon helicopter support. Major Alexia has been our inspiration since we were 6 and 4 years old. To become inspired, we must look around, watch what other people are doing, and see how they achieved their success and what inspires them. We were so lucky to have Major Alexia in our lives as her life is so cool, fun and filled with impact.

We are inspired by Alexia as not only is she an incredible leader, she is also a person who is so approachable and kind. She makes us feel powerful and empowered. She takes time out of her life to send us messages, encouraging us every step of the way and inspiring us to be someone like her who can save lives and make a difference. We got to know about Major Alexia through a children's book called "Alexia Learns to Fly" written by her mom Talia. She gave that book to our dad when she met him in at a military base. The book inspired us so much and since then, we have kept in contact. The children's book brings to life her story and how she wanted to fly as a little girl. This book inspires youths to chase their dreams and reach for the sky. We are grateful to say that we are two of thousands of youths Alexia inspires to this day. She has, and she will remain one of our biggest mentors in life.

Let us give you a typical example of an interaction with Major Alexia. It was a pleasure to have Alexia drop by our house on one fine day while she was in Toronto for a meeting. What made it so memorable is that she was with us from 5:00PM till 3:00AM in the morning. The time we spend together was genuinely inspiring and it was simply so cool to hang out with her. We had a fun time chatting about life at the same time learning valuable life lessons on how to confront fear, make your presence felt and go after your dreams.

To this very day, she gives us gifts from the Canadian Airforce, such as a jet plane-shaped candy, Airforce badges and the best of all, a pin of the yellow and red helicopter she flies to help people all across Canada. Alexia has established such an honorable career in the Airforce that she has received many awards.

With all these grand adventures and accomplishments, she doesn't forget the people in her lives. She takes time to remember those she is mentoring. Once Alexia was flying in British Colombia, and her view was a beautiful glacier with sparkling mist in the air. She sent us a picture with her colleague holding a cardboard that had "Hello Amna and Fatima" written on it. That picture meant so much to us as literally, she was teaching us how to fly, by being in the air herself with a glacier in full view and reminding us to remember others.

Moreover, she took a four hour flight to Toronto from Edmonton for the launch of Two Sisters on a Mission. It meant the world to us to have our role model fly in for our big day. She is now coming back for the launch of this book.

Rob Van Der Ende – Our friend and our mentor

Rob is a senior executive in FireEye and was previously the Asia Pacific Public Sector director for Microsoft. Rob is halfway across the planet, residing in Singapore but we feel his presence every step of the way. We talk to him before every major step in our journey and he always listens to us, offering us valuable advice but above all encouraging us. It means the world to us to know that a senior executive like Rob supports our vision and our passion. Just yesterday, we heard from him from Australia and before that from Indonesia and many other places.

Every time we talk to him, it is as if he is sitting right next to us and we are continuing our chat. Rob always takes action with us. He genuinely cares and it comes across in every interaction. We can proudly say Rob is one of those people who is always there for us, from flying halfway across the world for the business launch, to encouraging us right before going on Dragons' Den. He is flying in from Singapore to Toronto again to support our book launch!

Rob was also our first customer for a custom painting when he met Jason, our first nations artist, at the launch last year. The two connected as they shared a similar passion for life. Rob was so moved and placed an order for a custom painting. Jason was equally moved by Rob's ability to raise the spirits of others around him. Jason portrayed Rob's personality in the painting as a golden eagle. The painting is called Harmony and is dedicated to all role models that empower others.

In his own words, Jason describes the painting Harmony as follows, "The golden eagle is the role model landing on top of the tree representing the selfless people with their wings spread out sheltering the life under them. The tree is on an island of its own. There is a beautiful sunset with golden rays of light that are making themselves known, "This is the moment!!" There is nothing to fear as they are there, as the protector of this sacred tree, all life can continue to flourish and live. The tree is on a little tiny island surrounded by water like its own little oasis with just a tiny bit of mist. It represents a place where people feel blessed and indulge themselves to remind that life is a real beautiful place, and this is the place to be! We get to make our life a meaningful mission, and we get to choose what that means for us. There really is no limit to what's possible. We bring something different to the world just by being who we are. We can always count on sunshine or starry skies, rolling clouds or distant planets, beautiful chaos, or birds taking flight. There are lessons written all over the earth, all across the sky. On an island like this, there is a no prey nor there is a predator, as the role model is there to ensure equilibrium and protect the positive energy with strength and purpose. This painting Harmony is poetry in life, when color is unleashed and is set free, the most beautiful collaboration can occur, there is no predator and there is no prey! We can then come join hands and like nature, be sculpted to perfection. We shouldn't live our lives for tomorrow, we live it for today!"

Jason's words above really capture Rob's personality and why we really value him as a friend and mentor. He is like family to us now.

Maddie Babineau – The girl who gave her wish away

One of our most inspirational role models is a girl that we have never met but we feel her presence in the journey we are on right now. Her name is Maddie Babineau. We read her book about her cancer journey, and it truly inspired us.

After we had completed a keynote at one of the conferences, a lady named Sharon Babineau approached us and gave us a copy of her book about her daughter Maddie. Maddie story came into our life through her mom Sharon Babineau and inspired us deeply. She said that she felt the presence of her daughter in the room when we were speaking and that has never happened before. It was such a powerful moment for all of us. Sharon Babineau is a decorated military soldier, keynote speaker and author. Sharon's unique life experiences have taken her around the world and has formed the perspective and wisdom she now shares with others. Sharon served overseas in the first ever Canadian Military NATO trial of women in a combat service support unit.

The Children's Wish Foundation approached the lovely 13 year old Maddie Babineau after she was informed of her cancer diagnosis. They informed her, "You can have anything...a Disney cruise...the chance to meet your favorite star...a $5,000 shopping spree...anything." To those who knew her, it came as no surprise that none of those things were on Maddie's wish list. She knew exactly what she wanted. Maddie was filled with tears when watching a television program about the plight of orphaned children in an African village. Maddie's wish was to ease the suffering of these children who were half-way across the world from her. She wanted to see smiles on the children's faces. Despite her cancer, she initiated an incredible fundraising program for "her children."

We would recommend anyone who is looking for inspiration to read the story of this Canadian role model in the book "The Girl Who Gave Her Wish Away." This book tells us about her thoughts and her actions as she tries something that looked impossible at first. After reading the book, her story left a deep impression on our hearts.

In the book, Sharon reveals Maddie's remarkable journey, and emotions that led Maddie to provide hope and future prosperity to the village children. It is role models like Maddie and Sharon who inspire us to follow our dream and to truly share the message that anything is possible. We are so honored that Sharon is joining us at our book launch and bringing Maddie's bravery to life. See her videos and her story at www.maddieswishproject.com

Dr. Mike Allcott – We see far as we stand on the shoulders of giants!

Dr. Michael Allcott is an educator who truly empowers. Dr. Allcott has been an international educator for more than thirty years and has served in leadership roles at universities and colleges in Canada and the United States. His passion is for developing peoples' ability to build friendship and understanding across cultures. Dr. Allcott's career has included key positions like Dean of Sheridan International, Director of the Trent International Program and Head of Champlain College Trent University, and Associate Director of the International Centre at the University of Utah. Dr. Allcott has also taught at the University at Buffalo (SUNY), where he completed his PhD.

We met Dr. Mike a few days before we were going on Dragons' Den and obviously we were a bit nervous.

Instantly, he was able to inspire us by sharing how proud he was of our accomplishments, how the outcome didn't matter but the fact that we were showing up sends a message of empowerment to so many including him! What inspired us tremendously about Dr. Mike was that he just didn't give us advice but was able to come down to our level to truly raise our spirit. He even physically came down on one knee to take a picture with us as we were then the same height. As youths, these little gestures mean so much to us. He was using his power to empower us and show us that he believes in us.

Since that first meeting, Dr. Mike has been a key pillar of support for us and empowers us. From giving us his valuable time in meetings to having real business discussions with us. On a recent meeting at Sheridan College, he took us around the campus. What we learn from Dr. Mike is how good people use their power to empower others. How they don't just give advice and dominate the conversation, but really come down to the level of their mentee and lift them on their shoulders so they can see far.

Dr. Ulrich J. Krull – The Principal we love

Dr. Ulrich is the Vice President and Principal of University of Toronto Mississauga. Usually a trip to a school principals office is terrifying for any student let alone the principal of a university but Dr. Ulrich is one of nicest people we have ever met. We met him during a start-up event at University of Toronto where we had setup a booth. He dedicated over 30 minutes of his time going through our booth, our business model, listening to us, encouraging us and sharing how excited he was to see us give our dreams a chance. We were so inspired as we knew he was an amazing person and hearing those words from him meant the world.

Dr. Ulrich continued to support our journey and encouraging us in many different ways. Our most moving moment was when he invited us to sit in a meeting with the Executive Committee of the University when our dad was discussing the Experience Your Life Expo. To be surrounded by such incredible educators and to listen to the conversation really inspired us. To be very honest, the trust and respect that came with that invitation meant to so much and boosted us to really keep growing our dream. Dr. Ulrich remains a key role model for us and one whom we look forward to learning so much more from. He is definitely one has changed so many lives and is go grounded in his purpose that it inspires us to remain grounded in ours.

Karen Truyens – Education Industry Executive at Microsoft Canada

Karen has been a supporter, a customer and someone who has really encouraged us to go after our dreams every step of the way. From being the first one to encourage us after every post that we do on LinkedIn to being the first customer to support our book, Karen is literally with us every step of the way. As an executive for 25 years at Microsoft focused on Education, Karen is committed to unleashing the potential of youths through immersive learning and technology.

When we got the call from Karen that she and the team would like us to keynote the prestigious Microsoft Canada Digi Girlz event to over 200 high school students, we were so humbled and honored. It was an amazing day during which we saw that our story has the potential to inspire other people. It inspired us to write this book. We openly shared in our speech how ordinary we are and our story is not about us, but about the power of anyone who wants to make a real difference.

The best thing about Karen is that not only is she a senior account executive, she is one of the kindest and sweetest people we know. We always get messages from her individually and she goes out of her way to share our even most basic accomplishment. Knowing that a person like her who is so accomplished herself sees our passion and our drive is such a motivating experience for us. Being surrounded by Karen and other amazing technology executives has really inspired us to build our next business in STEM and we are working hard to learn the basics of introductory programming.

We are so grateful for role models like Karen and Dorothy (Practice Lead Microsoft) for their courage to blaze a path for girls in technology so we can follow in their footsteps. Their journey and their existence is inspiring us to really focus on making an even bigger difference.

Farah Perelmuter, CEO & Co-Founder Speakers' Spotlight

As we walked into the amazing office of Speakers' Spotlight, one of the top organizations in Canada, we could instantly feel two things. The first was positive energy that was in the space, it is hard to explain, but it was definitely there. The second was excitement as on the main screen were the words "Welcome Fatima & Amna Sultan". Meeting one of the most influential and inspirational businesswoman in Canada started with a bang!

Farah had heard our keynote at an event the week before and really encouraged us. When she talks and encourages you, you can tell how humble and grounded she is in her own life. She highlighted our strengths while never talking about her own accomplishments. She made us feel so special – started from having a pitcher of milk in her office for us for the famous 'cup of milk' conversation! We had talked about having a cup of milk over our business meeting as we were too young to have a cup of coffee but the purpose was the same. We definitely did not expect a full pitcher and it really meant a lot to us as she loved and cared for the fact that we were there.

Farah accomplishments are below, and they are absolutely incredible. However, we will speak about her energy and how she raised our spirits. For two hours, she gave us a detailed tour of her office, introducing us to the many people who make Speakers' Spotlight one of the best companies in

Canada. You can see the energy in the office was so positive and it really inspired us to see, very clearly, how a good business can indeed make a difference. One of our most moving moment was when Farah walked up to a closed door. She told us, that when she started her business, she struggled a lot for four year as any new business is hard to establish. She did not give up on her vision. Her only objective was to have enough client files that could fit a small filing cabinet. Her husband Martin and Farah worked really hard to achieve it for years. Then she opened the door and we could see a massive room filled with filing cabinets packed with files for thousands of events they booked their speakers for around the world. It was so moving to visually see what hard work and focus can do.

We also met Martin, Farah's Co-Founder and husband, who had built the business with her. As two sisters trying to have an impact as a business, seeing how two people can join hands to create something great was such an inspiration. Farah has been encouraging us to go after our dreams. Above all, her own journey of creating her own path is such an inspiration for us. We want to be just like her, not just successful in business, but successful in life by knowing that happiness is only in giving back. Since the very first year they started their business, in 1995, she has held annual fundraisers for various charities and have found ways to help those in need in their community and in various places around the world.

Farah shared her journey and how she overcame her challenges with us. Back in the day, marketing outreach was done by mail. She did not have the money to pay for the service so instead she brought a whole lot of envelopes and after inserting the flyers, hand closed them and delivered them across the neighborhood, door to door. Her openness to share the challenges that come with building a business was inspiring for us. It gave us courage that sometime when we doubt ourselves or feel the challenge, it is all part of the process. If we stay true to our mission and purpose, then anything is possible!

In terms of doing things that have not been done before, this role model really lived by that code. From humble beginnings in their apartment, they went on to do amazing things. Here is Farah's really impressive bio:

"Farah Perelmuter was born an entrepreneur. She started her first business when she was nine years old by performing at birthday parties (and being paid with cake). Her second big entrepreneurial success happened when she was 16. She had a flop in her early twenties, but it was followed by her best idea yet…Speakers' Spotlight. After graduating from the University of Western Ontario and completing a marketing program in Toronto, Farah began her career in the advertising industry.

In 1995, she took a deep breath and a major plunge into the biggest risk of her life. Along with her husband Martin Perelmuter, they quit their jobs and started their own business, Speakers' Spotlight. She became its CEO and Co-Founder, and he became its President and Co-Founder. Their adventure began.

Since beginning the business in a little room in their apartment, Speakers' Spotlight has grown beyond Farah's wildest dreams. It is now one of the world's largest and most respected speakers' agencies. They have arranged more than 28,000 speaking engagements in over 35 countries worldwide and have received many awards.

Today, the agency has offices in Toronto and Calgary, and the best staff in the industry. Speakers' Spotlight was selected by *Profit* Magazine as one of the 100 fastest growing companies in Canada, and Farah and Martin have been named finalists for the Ernst & Young "Entrepreneur of The Year Award" twice.

Farah has been featured in the media and recognized in the events industry numerous times. *Profit* Magazine ranked her as one of Canada's "Top 100 Women Entrepreneurs" for seven consecutive years, she was selected as one of "Canada's Most Powerful Women: Top 100" through the Women's Executive Network, and *The Women's Post* named her one of Canada's "Top 20 Women of the Year."

As we shared above, this chapter is our favorite as we highlight the amazing people who are supporting us and are literally the wind beneath our wings. Their presence is felt, and their sincerity powers us on. In addition to the list above, there are so many more people that we are grateful for and inspired by. Our role models inspire us not just with advice, but with their actions and existence. They are following their dreams and it inspires us to follow ours – no matter what obstacle comes in the way.

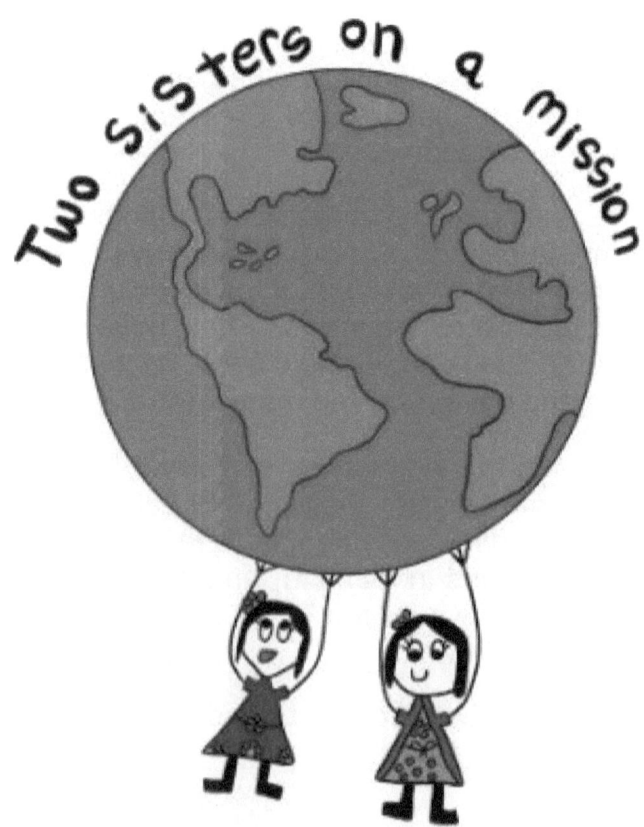

Major Alexia Hannam – The woman who taught us to fly

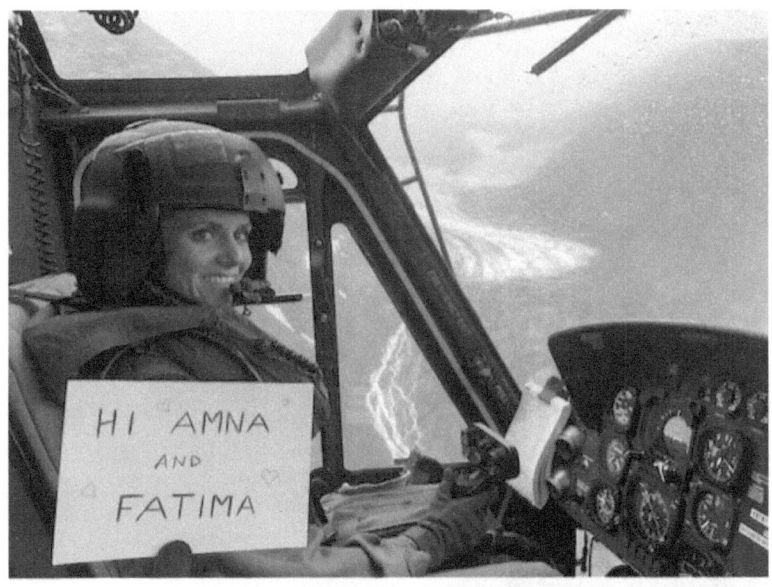

Major Alexia in her helicopter with a glacier at the back. The sign that said "Hi Amna and Fatima" really made our dreams fly!

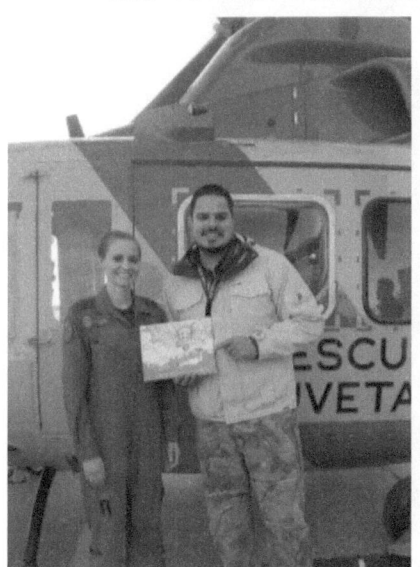 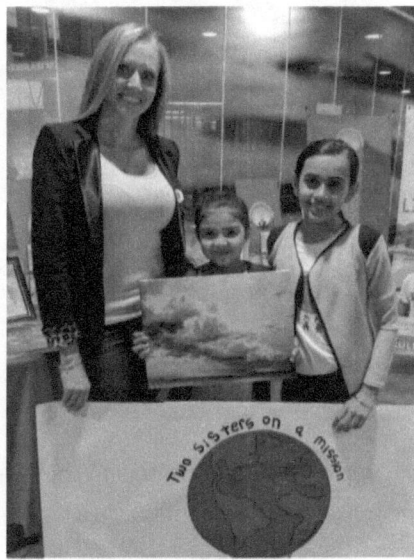

The moment when Major Alexia gave the book for us. Two years later, she took a four hour flight to be at our business launch in Toronto.

Rob Van Der Ende – Our friend and our mentor

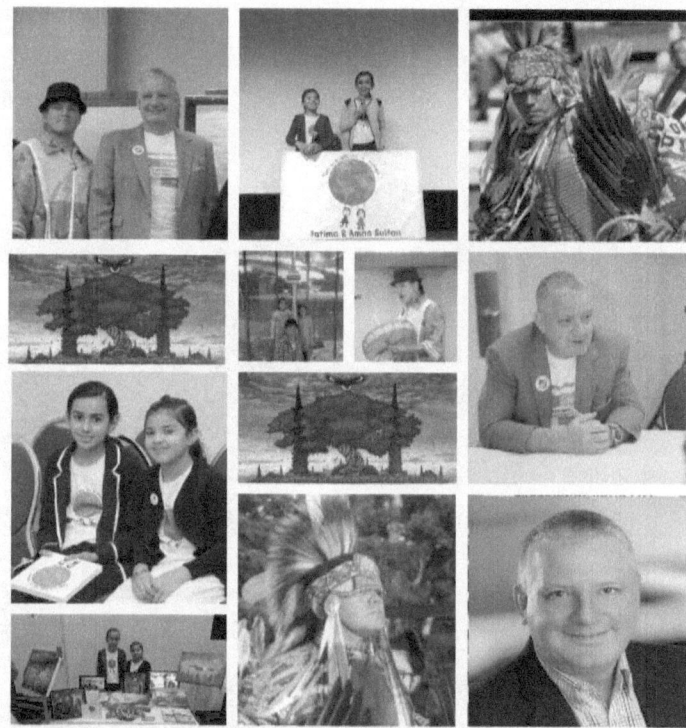

"As for our friend Rob's painting, I imagine a golden eagle landing on a tree and sheltering the life under him. There is nothing to fear as he is here, as the protector of this sacred tree and all of life can continue to flourish and live. The tree will be on a tiny island like its own oasis. It is a place that reminds that life is beautiful! Now try imagine this place...and I'll try and paint it!" Jason Fobister from First Nations of Canada
This frame is sent with LOVE to Rob from Fatima and Amna Sultan

This was a card for Rob for all the kind gestures he did for us. We sent it framed along with his custom painting. The painting in the center is 'Harmony' and it described in the next chapter.

Maddie Babineau – The Girl Who Gave Her Wish Away

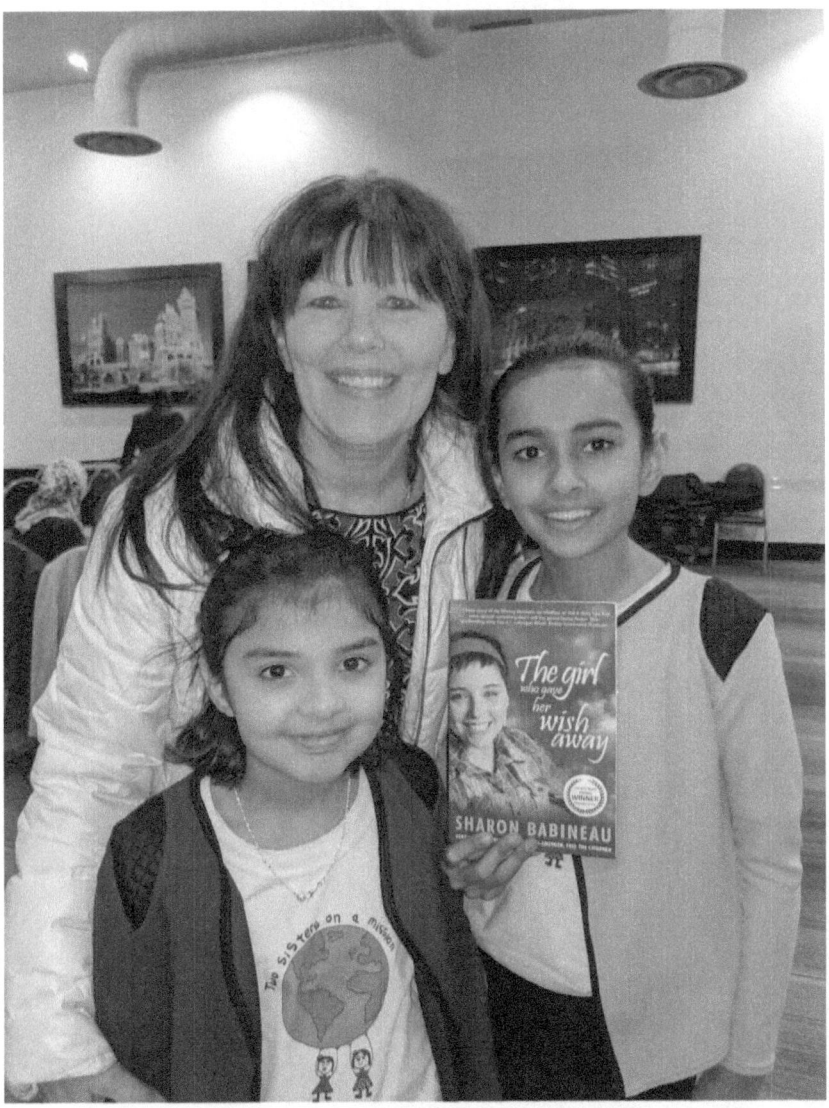

This is the moment we met Sharon and we are holding the book about Maddie. It truly inspired us.

Dr. Mike Allcott – We see far as we stand on the shoulders of giants!

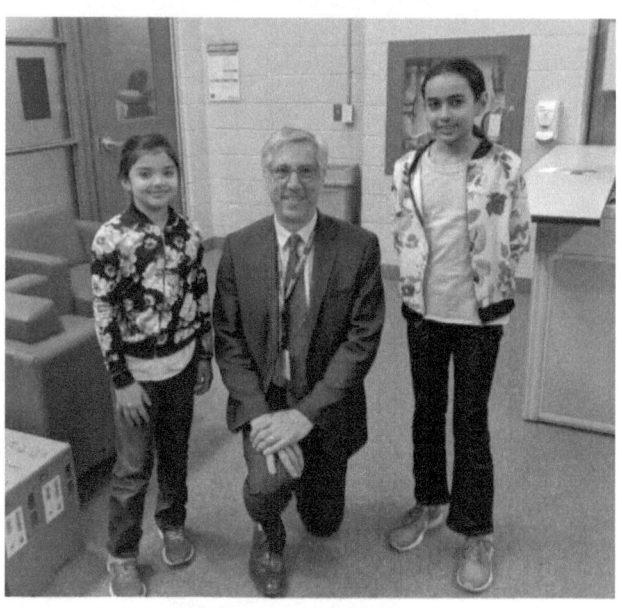

Days before going on Dragons' Den, we met Dr. Mike and he inspired us.

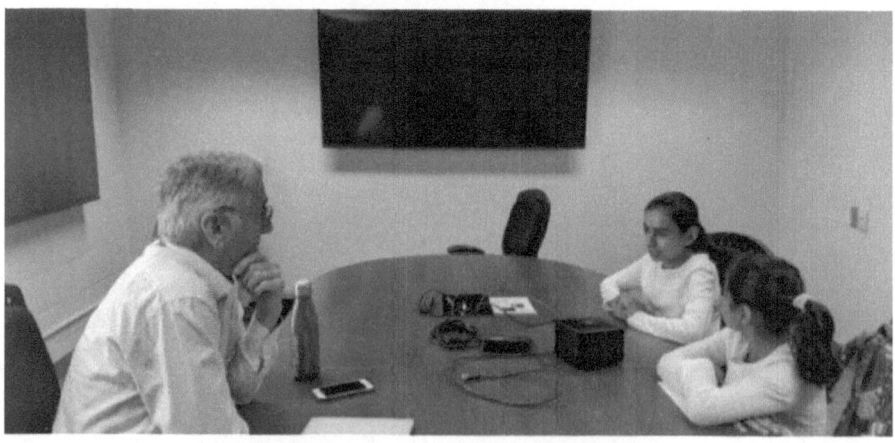

Dr. Mike always encourages us and takes our ideas seriously. This picture is from a meeting we had with him and captures how a role model truly inspires youths.

Dr. Ulrich J. Krull – The Principal We Love!

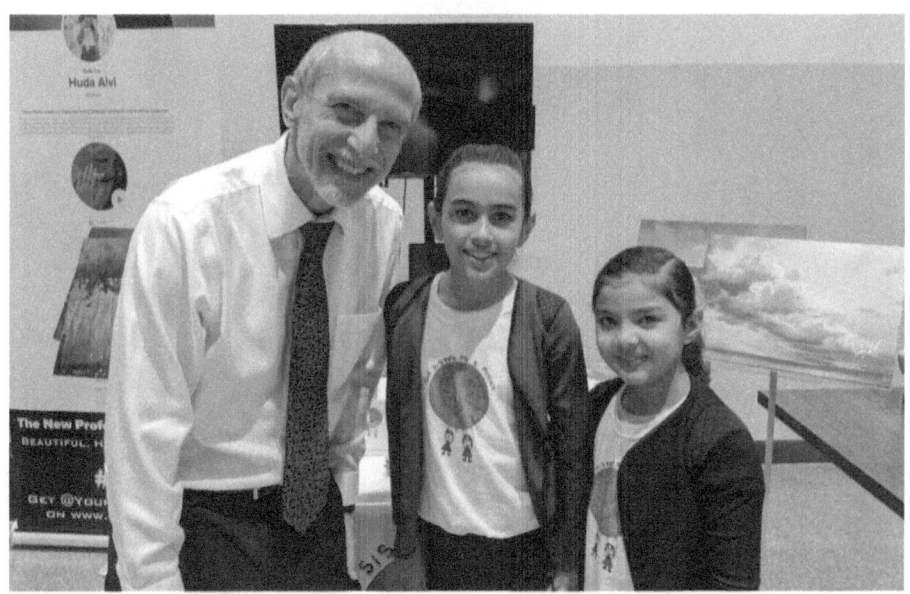

We met Dr. Ulrich J. Krull at University of Toronto Mississauga Startup Event. He spent 30 minutes at the Two Sisters on a Mission booth encourage us to go after our dreams. He is so kind and inspiring.

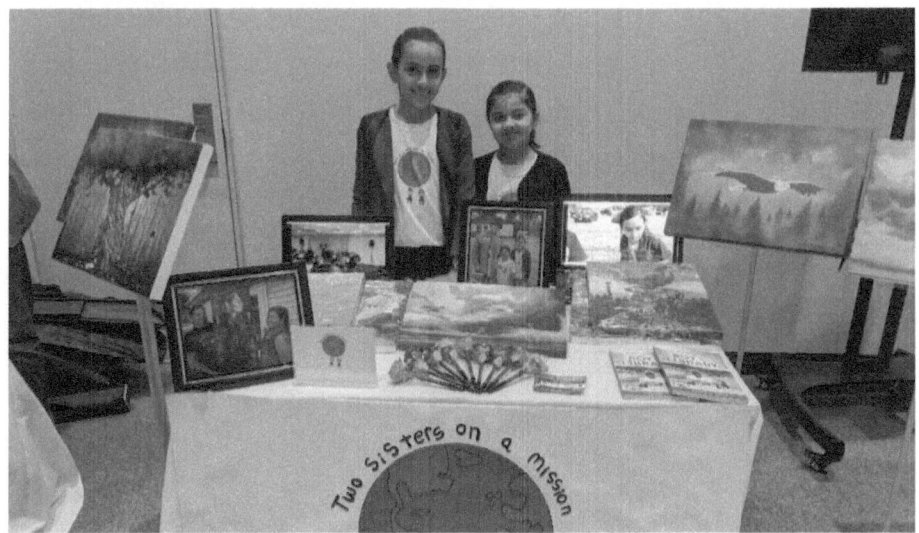

Karen Truyens – Education Industry Executive at Microsoft Canada

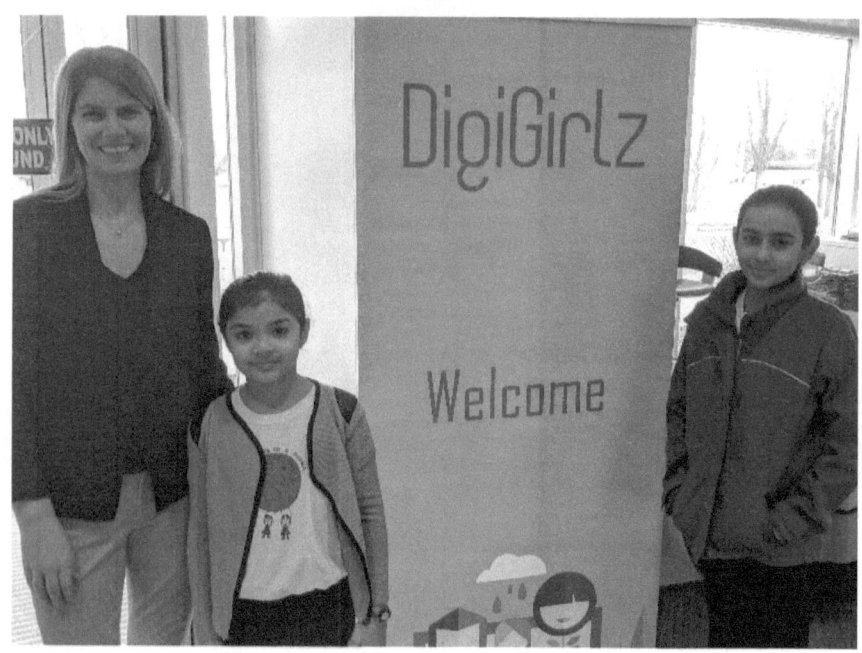

(Above) With Karen, right before our keynote at Microsoft Digi Girlz to 200 high school students. (Below left) Karen gave us an amazing tour of the Microsoft Office (Below Right) Karen when she received her first print from our store.

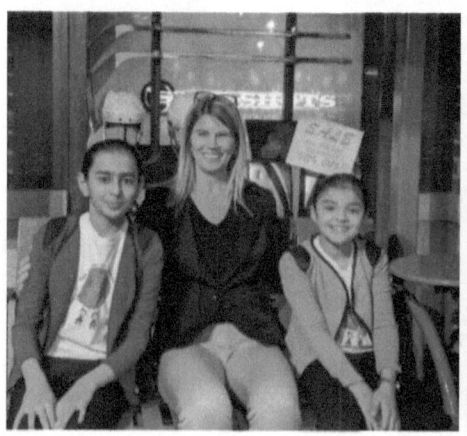
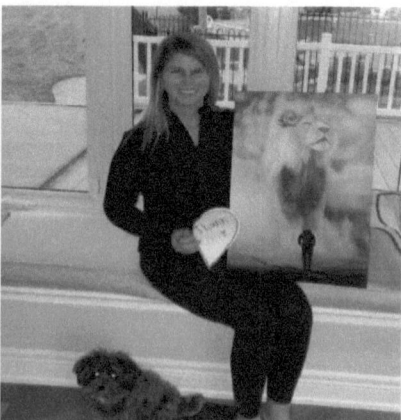

Farah Perelmuter, CEO & Co-Founder Speakers' Spotlight

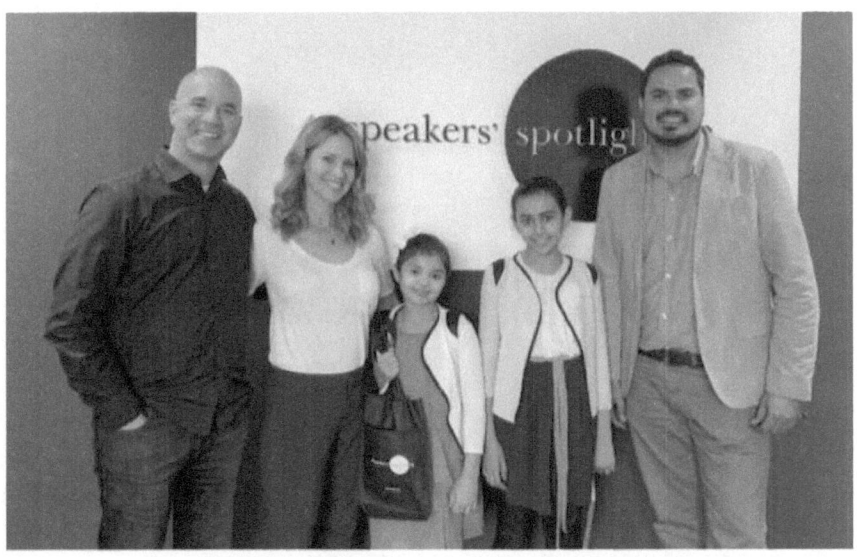

It was such a pleasure meeting Farah and Martin. We spent two hours with Farah and she was so real and kind. We are inspired to be just like her in life. (Below) Seeing our name as we walked in made us feel so special

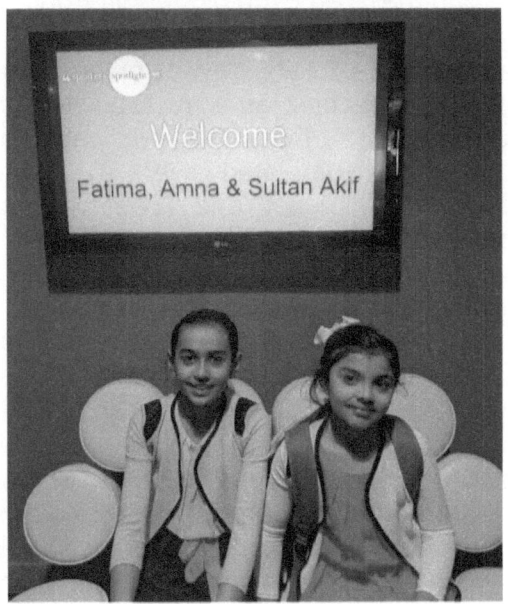

CHAPTER 10: INSPIRATIONAL ART

As a special feature, we are including the best paintings from our art store in this chapter. You will see why we fell in love with this art, the artist and their message once you see these pictures. They inspire us just as they will inspire you.

The world needs our collective action. We are on a mission to make a real difference and we look forward to work with you. There are several ways through which you can join hands with us so together we can make an even bigger difference:

1) Invite us as speakers to your event or organization. You can see some of our speeches at www.twosistersonamission.com under keynote speakers. At the time of publication of this book, we are honored to have completed over 40 keynotes in major conferences including Microsoft and Toastmasters. We are also thrilled to share that we are the keynote speakers for one of the biggest conferences in Canada in February 2020. Our message is focused on highlighting the power that exist in all humans once they connect with their purpose. It is a powerful message that the audience can relate to and it drives real change.

2) Purchase a print at www.twosistersonamission.com to support our mission and our artists. We would love to work with you to light up the boardrooms, corporate spaces and living rooms all across the world. We will be happy to work with you to produce a custom size print in any size or even an original painting.

3) If you have an event, a graduation ceremony or an award ceremony coming up that requires a large number of prints we would love to supply them for you in any size. We have been honored to provide prints for special events like graduation ceremonies and corporate events. We can produce these on canvas or on paper to match your budget.

Please email your requests to info@experienceyourlife.ca

Above all, we hope that you will take the message in this book and start a project of your own that you truly love. Through this book, we hope to drive real change so that others can take on the biggest problems in the world and help people. Through this book, we hope to start a chain reaction. We hope you will take action today to do something you have always wanted to do. When you feel that fear, remember, ANYTHING IS POSSIBLE!

From the Two Sisters on a Mission, we wish you love and happiness in your journey.

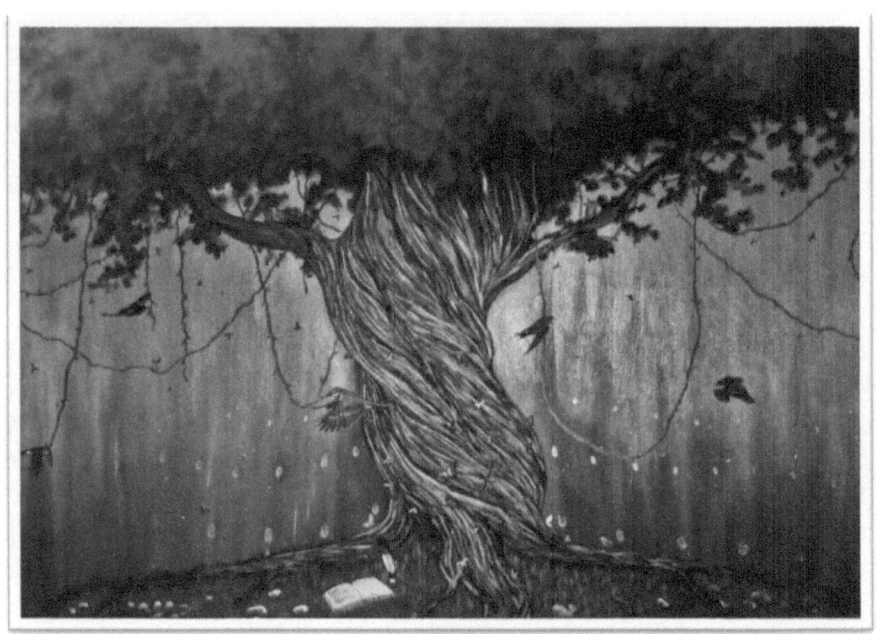

"LEARNING" - JASON FOBISTER

This painting is dedicated to all the mentors in our lives. It was inspired by the life story of a principal and the sacrifices educators make for their students. There was a principal who just loved teaching kids. In Jason's own words, "I was asked to paint for the farewell of this principal after teaching for 30 years and I didn't know what I was going to paint. His life story is pretty amazing, and I decided to paint a tree as it provides shelter to others. It had to be strong, and I started mixing my golds and my bronze colors. I could see the life of a teacher is so vibrant, so I painted the leaves red. I added a book in front of that tree because that is his life and his life is about teaching and helping people to learn. Because the tree is strong, life underneath it can flourish. I wrote a page in that book, and I left the other page empty. It is a symbolic reference that the story of life goes on for both the mentor and the mentee with positive energy all around it."

This is one of our favorite paintings and we have produced it in big and small sizes for our customers and events.

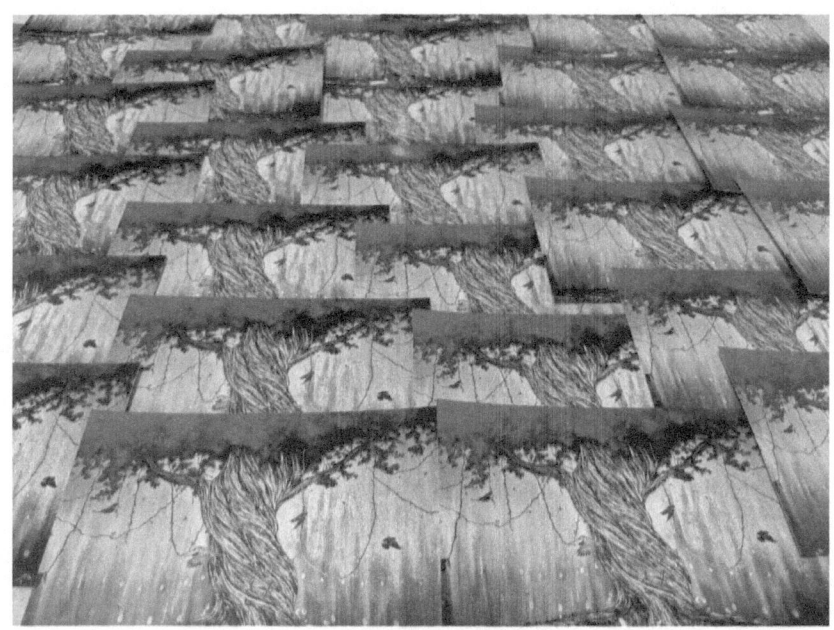

(Above) Our order for the graduating ceremony (Below) This was our biggest size so far. It was 9 ft by 5 ft.

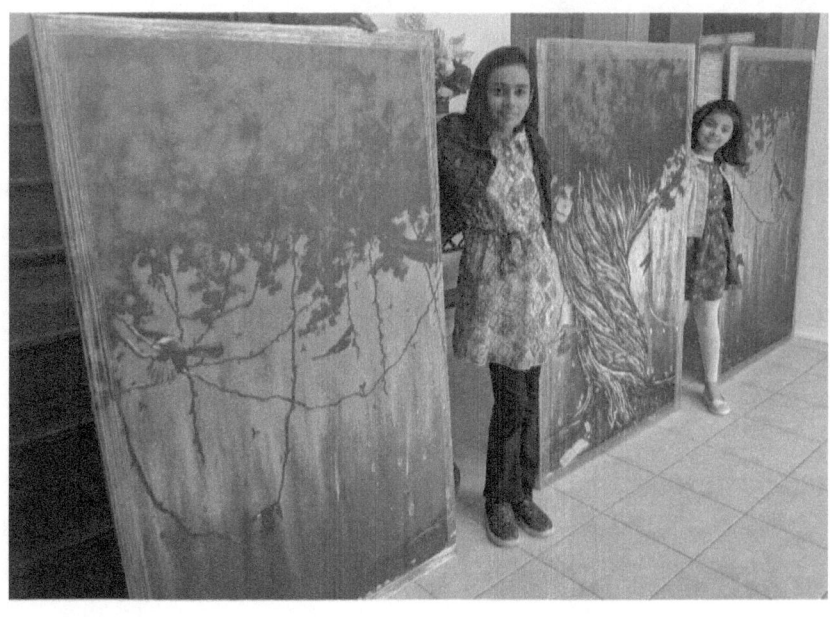

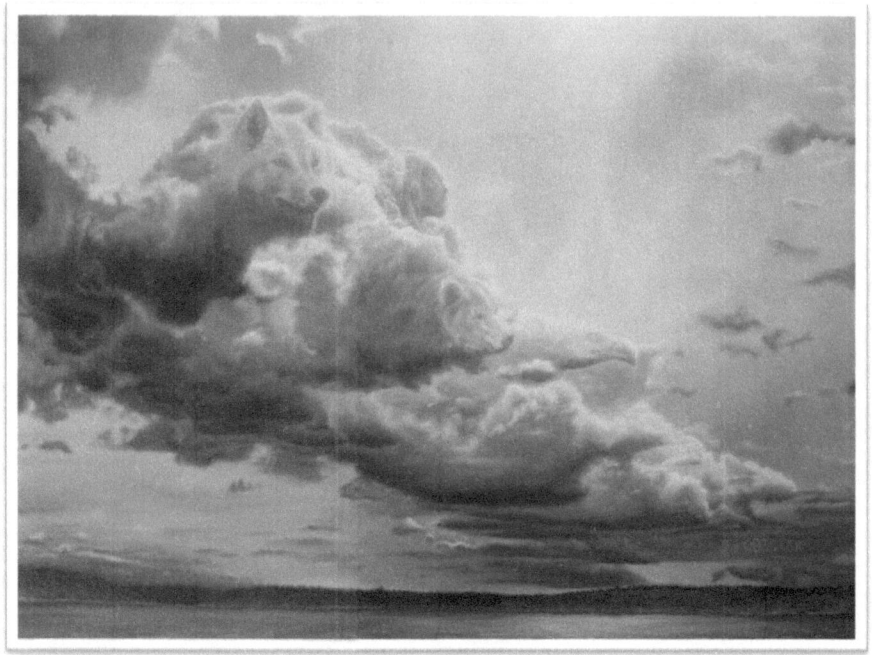

"WE ARE WARRIORS" - JASON FOBISTER

In Jason's own words, "One day I was looking across the lake from my home, when you look up the sky you can see shapes and the silhouettes of natural things you see in life. When I looked closer, I could see the shape of wolf, bear, eagle and a first nations warrior. After that the things started connecting and I drew what came to my mind. Moments like this in my life are the ones that are real and things of beauty. That is why I feel bad to put my name on the painting because it did not come from me but it came from life. It was something special for me because perhaps the creator helped me see that in life and to look for the lessons from life. The lessons come not just for me talking but they can come silently from nature and all you need to do is open your heart and mind."

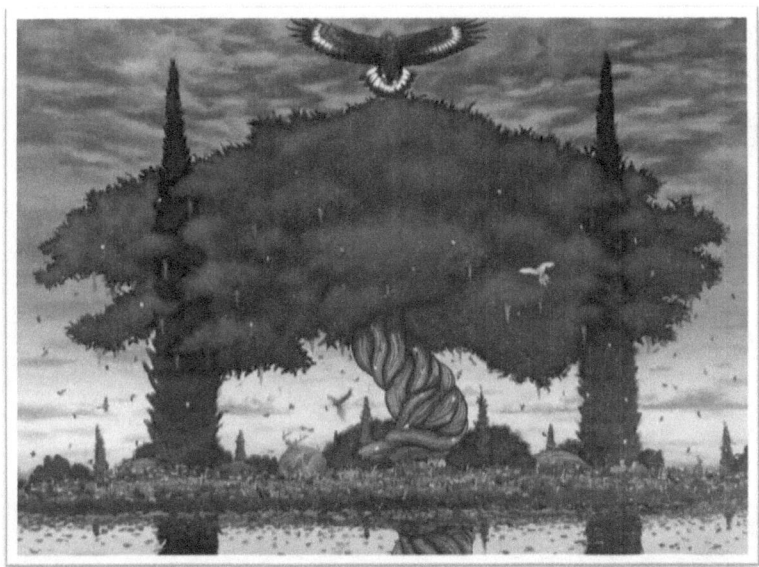

"HARMONY" - JASON FOBISTER

This painting is very special. It is our vision of bringing the world together come true. Our artist painted this for Rob Van Der Ende from Singapore after they both met at our business launch. It represents mentors and the selfless souls that support those around them. Rob flew in to support our event and has been a key mentor. Jason saw his personality and his purpose of using his strength to give power to others. He envisioned this painting in the following words: "The golden eagle landing on top of the tree represents the selfless role models with their wings spread out sheltering the life under them. With a beautiful sunset with golden rays of light that are making themselves known that this is the moment!!! There is nothing to fear as they are there, as the protector of this sacred tree, all of life can continue to flourish and live. The tree is on a little tiny island surrounded by water like its own little oasis with just a tiny bit of mist. And I think that is the place people feel blessed and reminded that life is a real beautiful place and this is the place to be! This painting Harmony is poetry in life, when color is unleashed and is set free, the most beautiful collaboration can occur, there is no predator and there is no prey! We can then come join hands and like nature, be sculpted to perfection. We shouldn't live our lives for tomorrow, we live it for today! "

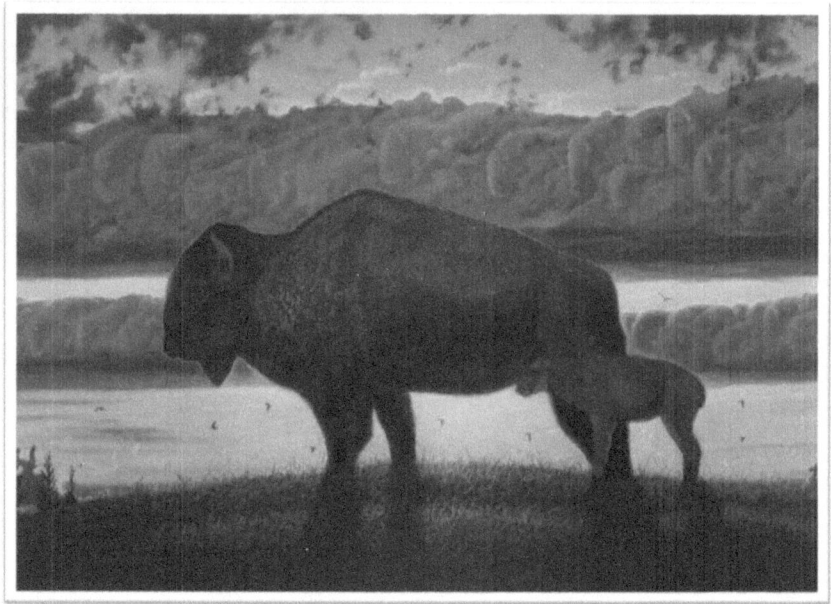

"STAND TALL LITTLE ONE" - JASON FOBISTER

In Jason's own words, "For those times when you stand for something you believe in against all odds, remember you are not alone. You stand on behalf of those that stood before you. You stand for a movement, for courage and for giving a voice to the sacrifices of those before your time. Look carefully at the clouds and the true meaning of the painting will reveal itself. You will see the herd of buffalos in the clouds. The wise buffalo passes on the lesson of courage and character to the little one just as it had that message passed on to it by other generations. He whispers softly to the young one, Stand Tall Little One - For Those That Came Before You. You stand for something that is bigger than you individually".

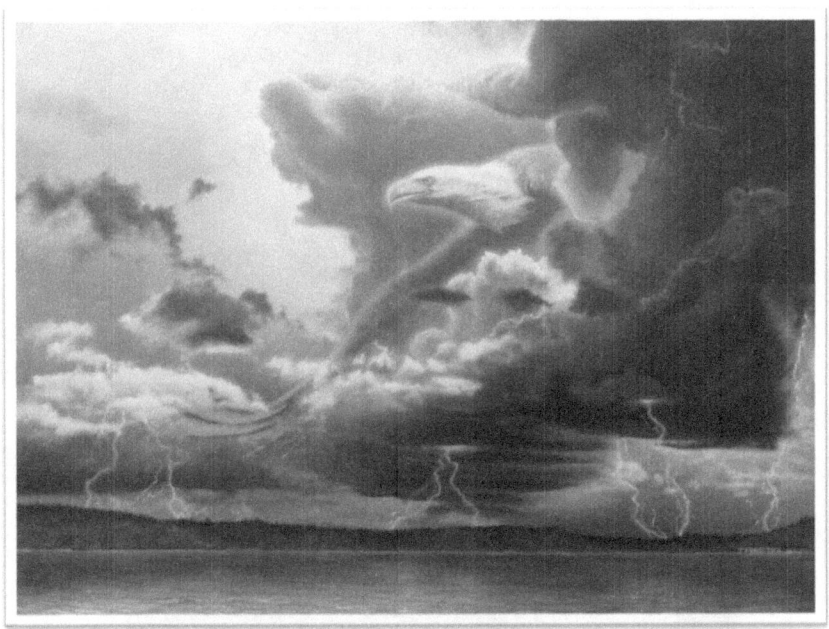

"THE ARRIVAL" - JASON

In Jason's own words, "The Arrival - I spoke against harmful things when I was 18 as I had friends who were getting involved in things that will harm them in life. I spoke about it in school and someone said that we should recognize him as there is something special about him.

So, during that ceremony, I had a vision that I was an eagle flying from the west over a lake and by the time ceremony was over, they told me that my spirit sits in the east and I look out towards the west. So, I saw my spirit coming from west to come meet me. Having a pipe (First Nations award) is a privilege given to you to carry for people and to understand life more closely. It gave me the opportunity to pray and to learn to pray. Life is not just air and rocks, there is a spiritual side to life. Everything is made up of energy and everything is attracted towards that energy."

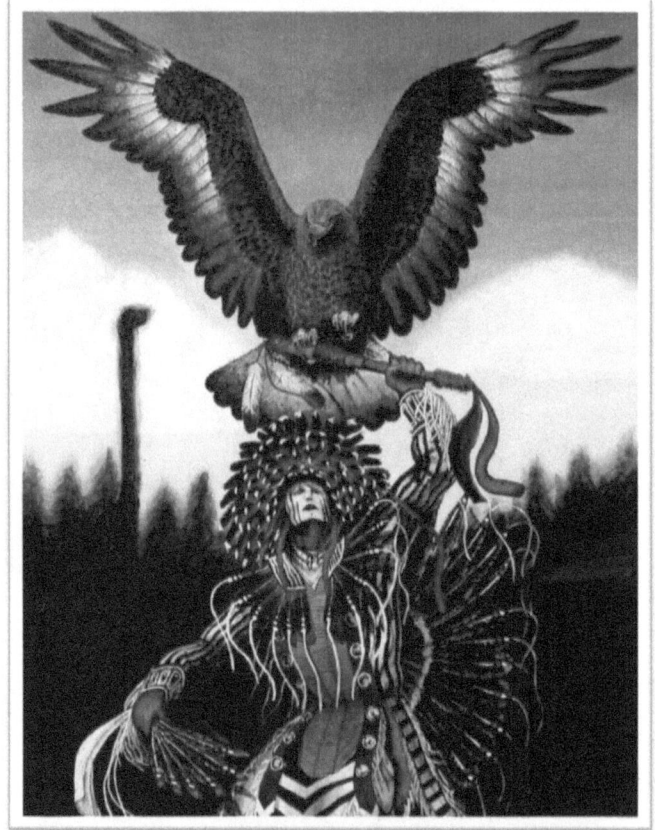

"THE MESSENGER" - JASON

In Jason's own words, "When a traditional dancer dances, people always see his power and steps and how he is dressed. They are very fierce and brave but, they have a beautiful dance. When he grabs his whistle, it is a part of the eagle's wing. The significance of the eagle whistle is to pray for people. When you blow that whistle you are giving the eagle life again because you're with the eagle and it is not all by your self. The painting to me has a lot of power because he is holding the eagle on his staff, he is looking at it. He has so much grace and power that for the rest of his life he is going to be a dancer. That is what the dancer is doing he is bringing back to life to an animal which had a past, and he is giving life to people who observe him dance."

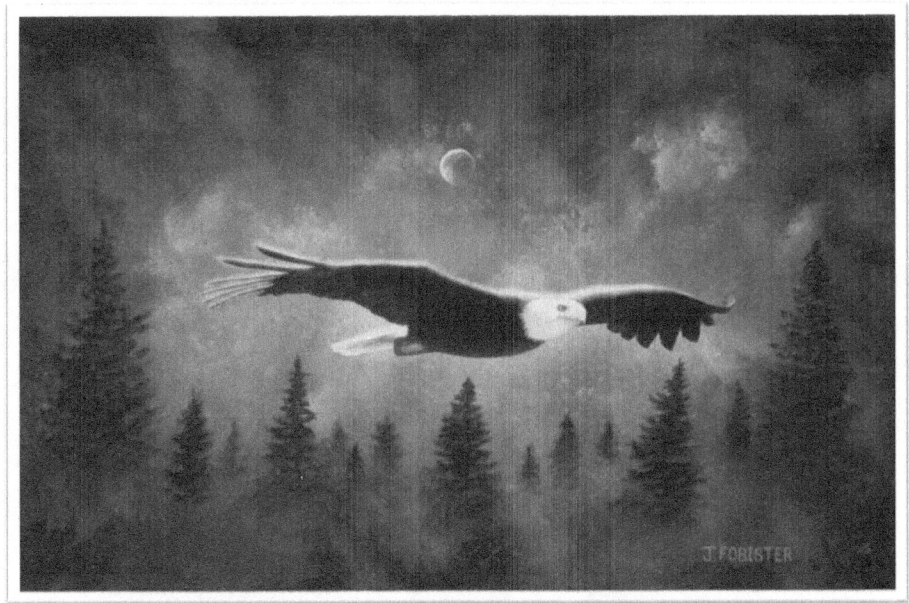

"EAGLE DREAMS" - JASON

In Jason's own words, "Not every mistake is a bad experience, this painting is an example of that. I had an idea in my head and I pursued it. I painted an eagle with a moon in the background, but I accidentally put too much water on my brush and it dripped on the canvas. I was thinking "oh no" and then I grabbed a rag and tried to wipe it but it made streaks on the painting. It had such a unique quality that I didn't want to fix that mistake instead I wanted to use that mistake and make something good of it. That mistake was actually the best thing that happened to that painting. So later, I added more drops and ended up wiping it, adding more color. It was real joy doing that painting. You can always learn from mistakes. They don't hurt as long as you can find beauty in it you can always do something with it. Don't always go with your original plan because plans always change. This painting was proof of that and something I can learn from."

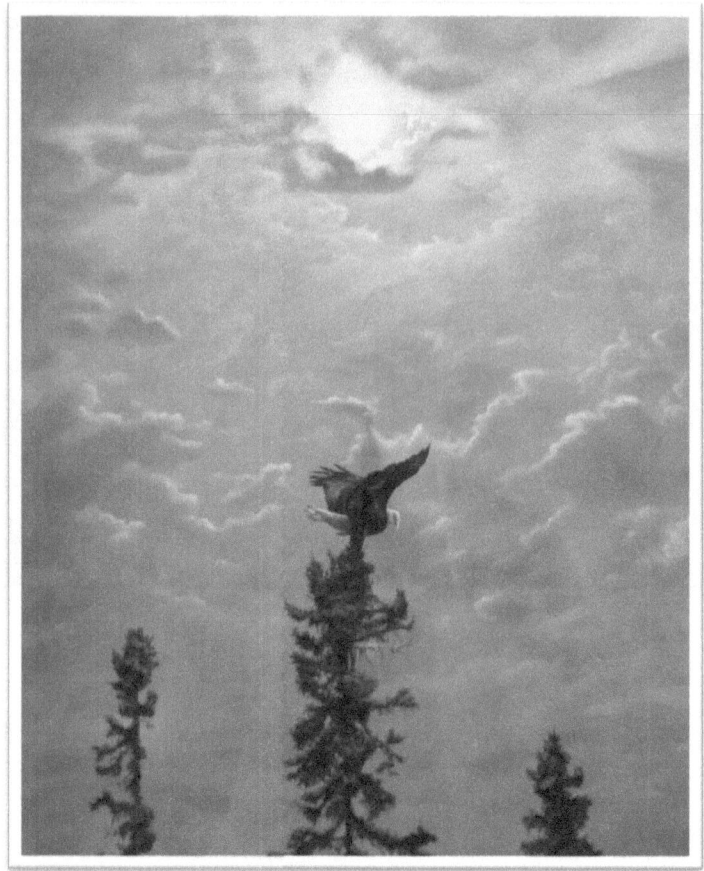

"POWER AND RESPECT" – JASON FOBISTER

In Jason's own words, "One time I was fishing and saw an eagle. Sometimes if you catch a fish and you throw it back in the lake a eagle might come and take it. So that is what I did and then an eagle came and took it to the top of a tree.

Then I started to fish more and caught another fish and threw it to. Then an eagle came and took it but, I had gotten my camera and the eagle had landed on the perfect tree. I really wanted to capture the grace and the power when it landed on the tree and he had my fish and in that moment we were connected"

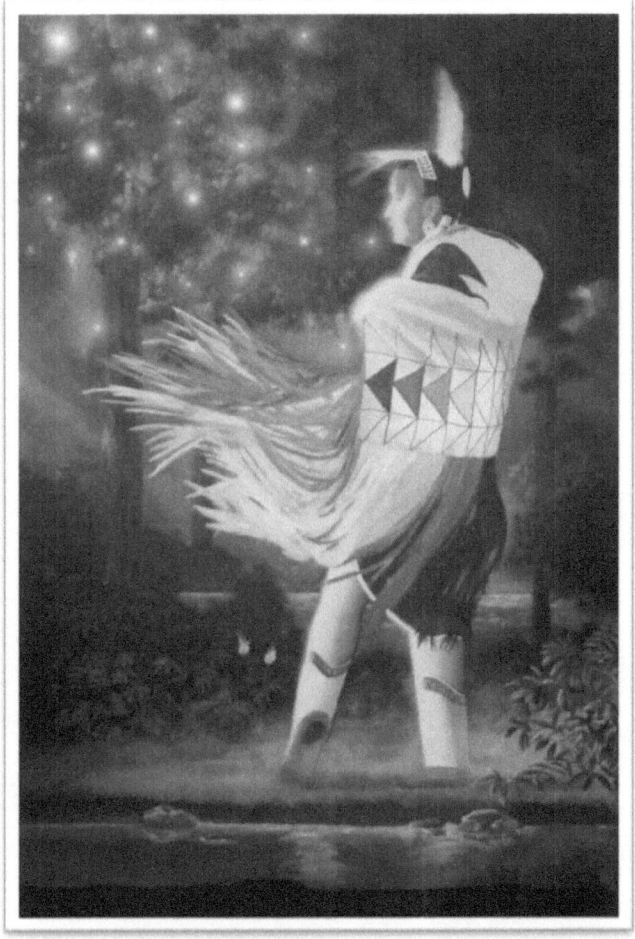

"FANCY SHAWL BUTTERFLY DANCER" - JASON FOBISTER

In Jason's own words, "This dance is called the butterfly dance. The dancer is vibrant and alive when it flutters. It is very beautiful to watch the colours move the way they do and there is a lot of strength in the dance. That is what the fancy shawl dancer is about. It is about the butterfly protecting the dancer and that dancer is honoring the butterfly. There is balance and beauty. The power, the beauty and the grace of the butterfly dancer is what I wanted to capture in this painting."

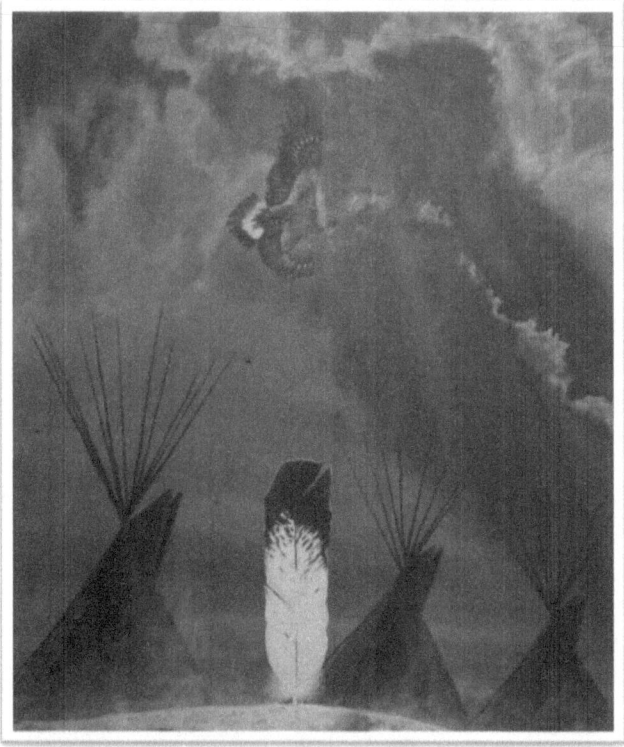

"THE GIFT" - JASON FOBISTER

In Jason's own words, "In first nation culture, the eagle is a messenger in our culture because he can fly high and talk to the creator. This is a representation of a traditional story. There was once this man who was sick, and he had powers to talk to animals. He goes to the beaver to climb the tree and pass on his wishes to the Creator. The beaver goes and comes back with a bear, the man asks if the bear could climb the tree and talk to the Creator. The bear says I cannot do that, but I have a friend who might and comes back with an Eagle. The eagle says that I can only fly to a limit, but I will try, so it flies out into the sky and goes close to the Creator and delivers the wishes. The Creator send a gift to the man in the form of a feather. If you notice in the painting closely, there is a feather missing. The whole painting is in colors that capture the spiritual nature of this story."

ANYTHING IS POSSIBLE

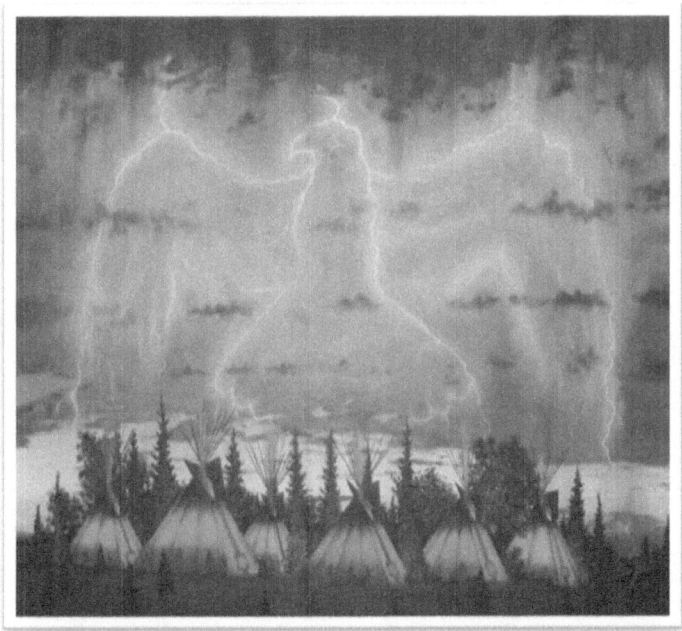

Visit www.twosistersonamission.com to see the full catalog including the following prints and videos from our artists.

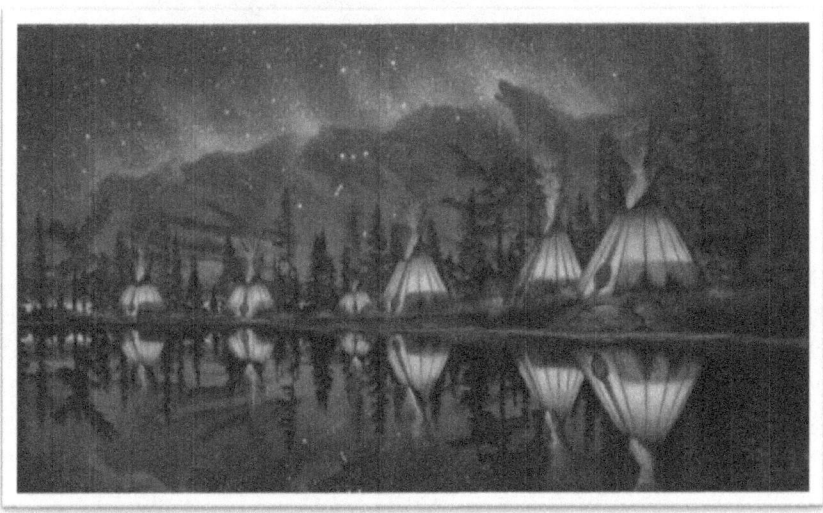

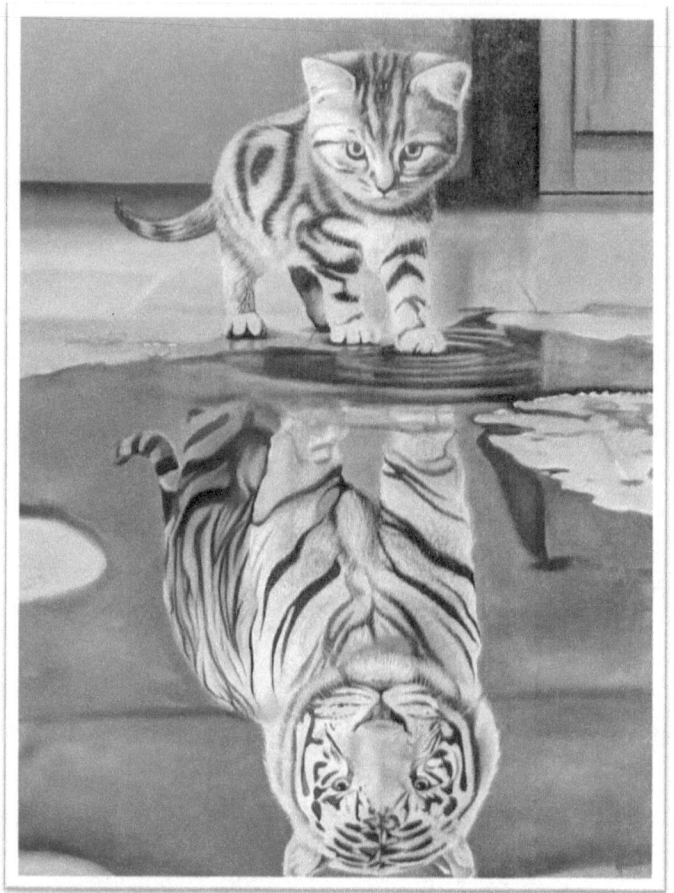

"COURAGE" - DAVIEL GALAN

This art moved us personally as well. We may be small, but we have big dreams. We may be young, but our business model is strong. We may be youths but just like any other youth, we have the power to change the world. We dedicate this painting to all the youths of the world, to help them realize, they have within them the power they need to make a difference. To all the youths out there, this art is for you. Never underestimate the change you are capable of making in the world

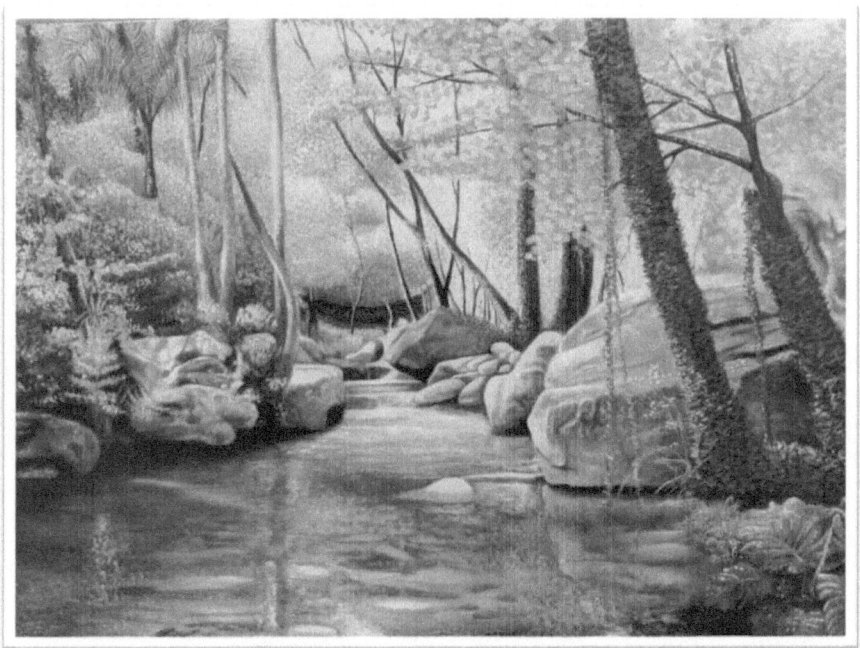

"REFLECTION" - DAVIEL GALAN

Daviel knows how to write and read braille. When we asked him what his favorite painting means, he told us that this painting is explained in braille on the bottom right corner of the painting. He then closed his eyes and read what it had said using this fingers to read the braille. It was about calmness that can only be achieved from within. That moment was so moving for us. The different shades of green in the painting is truly amazing, so is the story behind it.

Can you see the eye in the painting? It is closed and in the center. The painting is encouraging us all to feel and not just to see. Now on the bottom right hand side is the description of the pictures in braille. The painting reflection encourages us to calm down and know that we all have the ability to feel this calmness.

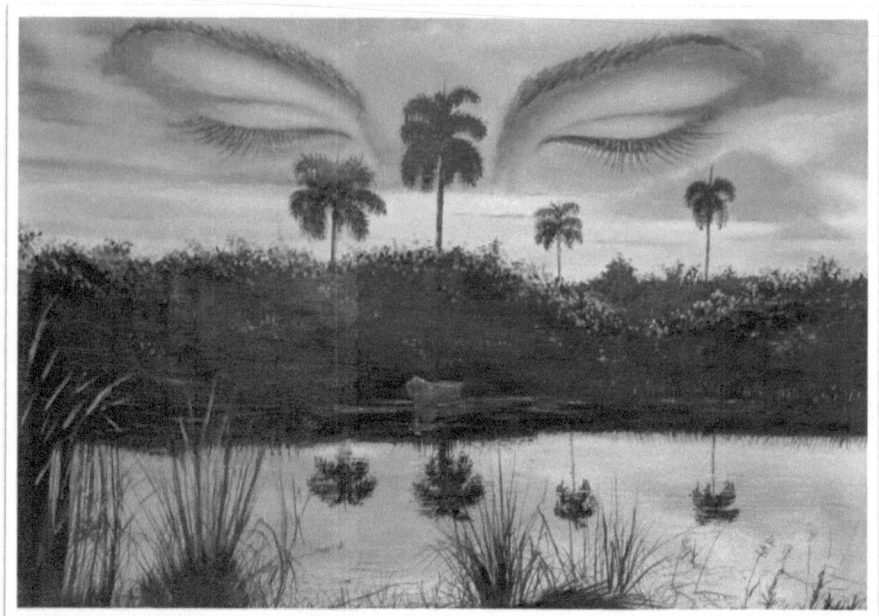

"HOPE" - DAVIEL GALAN

The sunset marks the end of a day but it always marks the point where there is hope for another day of new beginnings and of new emotions.

This painting is also expressing the artists love for those that have visual impairment. While they may not see the sunset, they feel it. They feel it sometimes a deeper level than those that see it. It is lesson for all of us to have hope, to not just see things but to feel them.

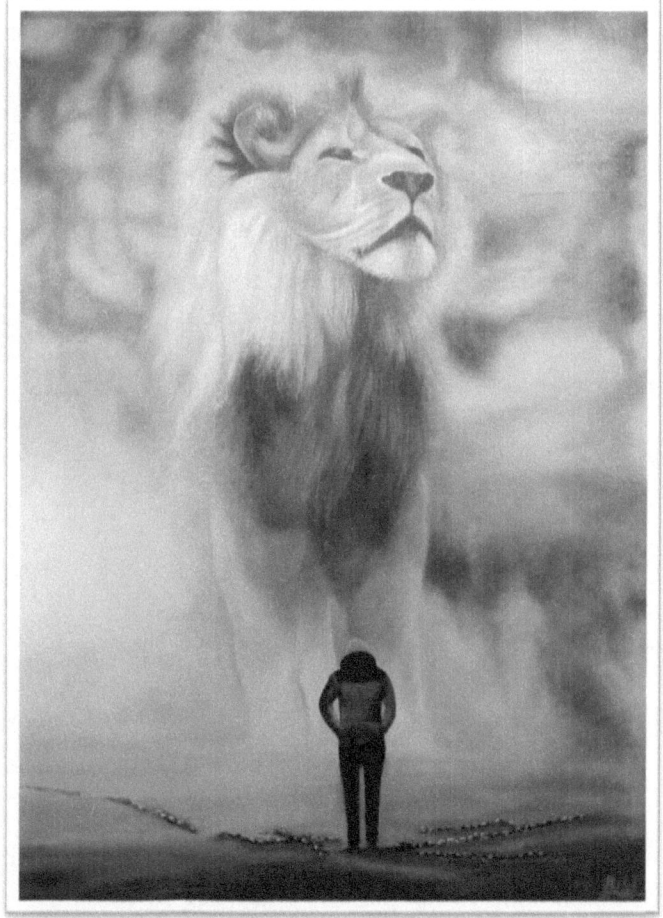

"FAITH" - DAVIEL GALAN

We sat down with Daviel and talked about doubts that surround all change makers. They are like chains. Shackles of fear. As change makers, we all have the power to break them. We have the power to rise. We have bigger forces looking after us and we do not have to feel limited anymore. The biggest failure is when we do not try. Daviel was in the process of painting this masterpiece and included broken chains to represent the journey of a change maker.

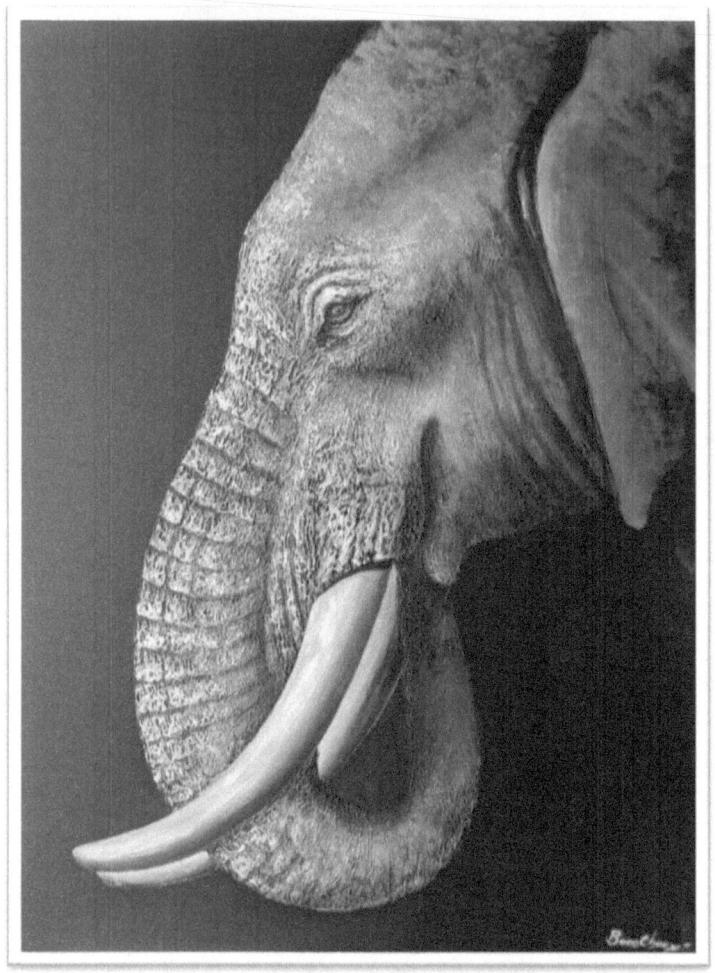

"GENTLE GIANT" BY BOON CHOO

Her art is so expressive that it doesn't need an explanation. This painting, Gentle Giant, represents the amazing souls who go through life calmly but with a strength that is incredible. Their presence brings peace to those around them but at the same time, they are really strong but don't use their power to make others feel less.

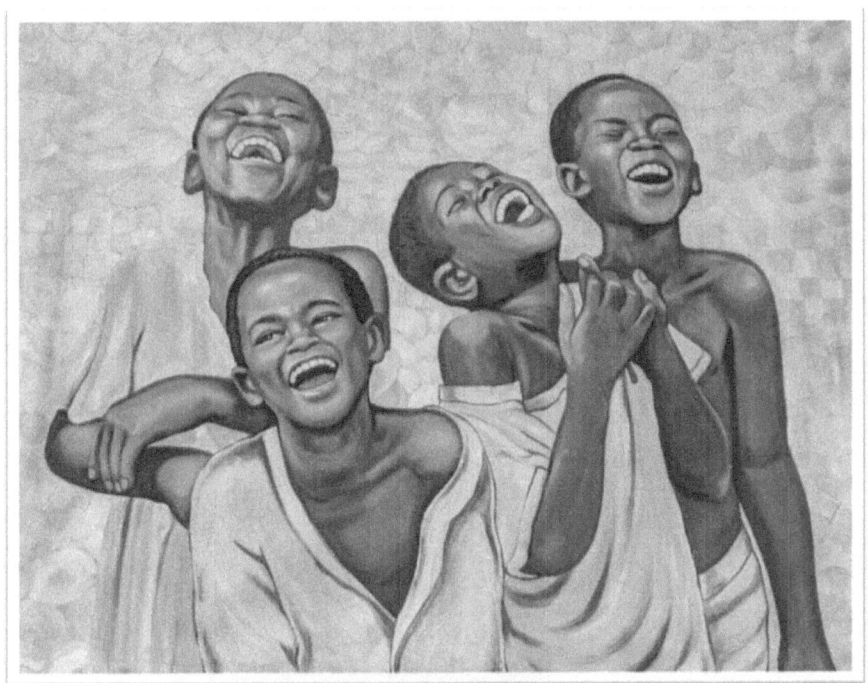

"JOY" - YASMANI HASAN

This is one of our favorite paintings and we actually got to paint a little bit of it with our artist. The painting captures children from Africa that are having an amazing moment. Children from Africa are always represented in malnourished and sad images. His message is that they too have happy moments and can teach us all a lot about being grateful and enjoying life with limited resources. We personally experienced this with other children our age during the library building trips. This is one of our favorite paintings. The laughter is the painting is just so real and the joy comes out of the painting to lift the space in which the painting exists.

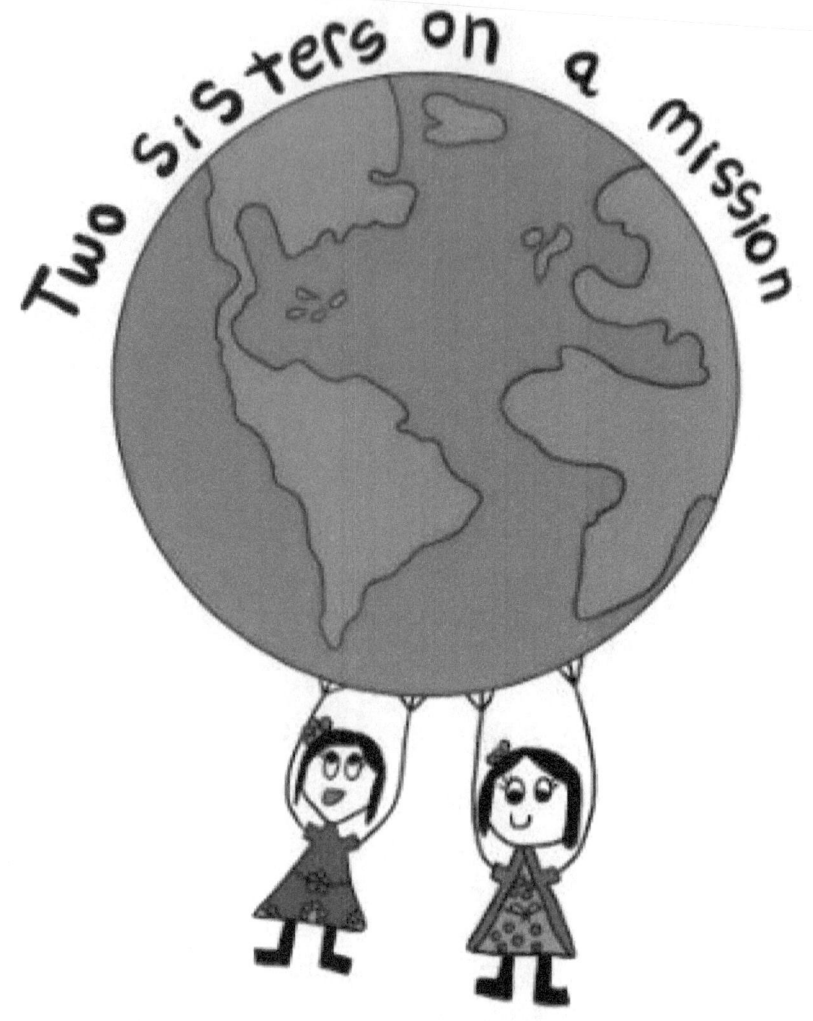

www.twosistersonamission.com

Join hands with us to make an even bigger difference together.

www.ingramcontent.com/pod-product-compliance
Lightning Source LLC
Chambersburg PA
CBHW031414210526
45464CB00005B/1879